BEYOND THE BACK ROW

BEYOND THE BACK ROW

THE BREAKTHROUGH POTENTIAL OF DIGITAL LIVE ENTERTAINMENT AND ARTS

JIM McCARTHY

HOUNDSTOOTH
PRESS

For my friends and colleagues
working in the live entertainment and arts world,
past, present, and future.
But especially…
for those who were there in March 2020.
You kept the light on.

CONTENTS

INTRODUCTION

I admit it. I was a Covidiot at first, but I blame Stephen King.

It's not fair to Mr. King, but it's true. It took me a moment to grasp what COVID-19 was going to do to us all because I'd read too many of his books.

Allow me to explain.

It was January 2020, and I was at a roundtable dinner with a high-ranking public health official in Los Angeles County. Our topic: this virus.

You know the one. It was in China and a few other places in the far east. The pictures were spooky enough: whole cities shut down, empty highways, abandoned sidewalks in what would usually be bustling neighborhoods.

Scary. Eerie. So much so that it had a sci-fi vibe to it, but not just any sci-fi vibe. It reminded me of a famous book that also happened to be about a virus—Stephen King's *The Stand*. The story is about a virus that starts small, but by the time it's done, it has killed 99 percent of the world's population.

This dinner gave me a chance to learn how concerned I should be directly from a health expert. It was still early in the pandemic, and we didn't know all that much.

"So…is this Captain Trips?" I asked. "Captain Trips" was the name of the virus in the book. I figured an epidemiologist would know that.

"Do you mean is this a slate-wiper?" she said.

"Yeah, is this a slate-wiper?" I asked. That sounded even worse somehow. At least, Captain Trips sounds fun and adventurous. A little gallows humor in the midst of the end of the world.

"No, it's not a slate-wiper," she said. "Let me break it down for you."

And then I learned what we would all learn soon enough. She explained the virus was easier to catch than the flu AND more deadly. Not only a little bit either. Put a five- or ten-times multiplier on each of those numbers and you've got the idea.

Oh my. That is serious, I thought.

For a short time, though, my relief that we weren't facing the end of the world clouded my judgment. It didn't sink in what it would mean to have something 25 to 100 times worse than the flu going around.

The next day at work, I stared at the sales report for a big touring musical we were promoting. Great numbers. Thousands of people clamoring to go.

And in that moment, it all came together in my mind.

I saw the empty freeways and entertainment districts of China again in my mind's eye. No, we weren't all going to die, but if we didn't rethink all our normal ways of doing things, a lot of people would.

I had a special stake in this problem. If nobody's driving around or going to restaurants, they're not going to events either. Concerts, plays, musicals, comedy clubs, magic shows, escape rooms, baseball games—they'd all stop.

Of course that was a problem for me as the co-founder and then-CEO of Goldstar. We've been in the business of selling tickets to live-entertainment events since 2002. We're an online business, but the end product is not online. We built a live-entertainment marketplace for live producers to find audiences. We invented the concept, and we do it well. We've sold tens of millions of tickets to millions of people for thousands of venues. Maybe you've bought tickets from Goldstar, and if so, thank you! Glad to be of service.

Of course, our business relies on shows actually happening. COVID-19 seemed almost purpose-built to shut us—and the rest of the industry—down.

In February of 2020, I asked our customer service team to track the number of customers they engaged with who had coronavirus-specific concerns. Each day, we tallied the customers with questions or worries related to the virus and those who wanted refunds because of it. At first, the numbers were low. One or two per week. Then one or two a day. Then four. Then ten. Then twenty-five.

Uh oh, I thought. I knew where this was going.

Soon, it was the only question we were getting from customers. Not long after that, I sent an email to 10 million customers. It started, "I can't believe I'm saying this, but I don't want you to go out to live entertainment right now."

It was Friday, March 13, 2020. The live entertainment industry in North America was about to shut down completely. We didn't know when it would reopen, but we knew it wouldn't be soon.

I wrote this book for those who want to succeed with online events. The possibilities of this new medium are endless, and I want to share what I've learned with you.

I wrote this especially for my colleagues and friends in the industry who went through the pandemic shutdown. For those who fought hard to survive. For those who want the future to be bigger than the past.

In May of 2020, we greenlit Stellar, now the gold standard for people serious about online events and digital live entertainment. By August, we had a beta product, paying audiences, and real shows. By

December, Stellar had hosted hundreds of events, including *Jagged Live in NYC*: A Broadway Reunion Concert, the first real, live, on-stage performance of Broadway content since the pandemic started.

This story, though, isn't about us, and it isn't about the past. It's about you, and it's about the future. My goal is to get your feet on the ground and enable you to start reaching for the stars. To do this, I'm going to cover three things:

1. *Why* you should produce online events.

2. *How* to produce online events.

3. *What* kinds of online events you can and should produce.

This book is for everyone responsible for producing or marketing live entertainment and arts. That includes people with a lot of different job titles. Music promoters, executive directors of theatre or arts nonprofits, theatre producers, venue owners, artists or artists' managers, heads of marketing for organizations big and small, and live-entertainment entrepreneurs all fit, as do many others. Depending on your exact role and the size of your organization, some of the information in this book may be more directly relevant to the work you do or oversee, while other parts may be indirectly or less relevant to your specific position. Still, I wrote this as a primer, not an encyclopedia. For example, even if you're not involved in the technical aspects of a production, you will still benefit from understanding the parts of this book discussing them. Non-marketers should read the marketing chapter. I feel strongly about this because digital live events are a new medium, and the rules are still forming. Now is the time to have a broad understanding of what's happening, what's the opportunity, and what's coming.

WHAT TO EXPECT

This book is a primer to enable you to understand what online events are, how to get everything you can out of them, and where to start in this new space. It's not a technical how-to manual or a book of marketing tricks. On the other hand, if you know nothing at all about online events when you begin reading this book, you'll be ahead of 95 percent of the people in the industry when you finish it. And you can grow from there.

Here's an overview of what you'll learn:

- The new possibilities online events create

- The ways in which online events make success in live entertainment easier

- How online events extend your reach to new places and audiences

- How online events can make you a star in your organization or industry (or just make you a star!)

- How to future-proof your career and skills

- How to maximize your chances of success and reduce your risks

- The right mindset for online events

- What the future holds for online events and the rest of the live industry

This book is meant to help you make some leaps. This new medium of digital live entertainment is still taking shape, and the opportunities are wide open.

Do you want to do fascinating work? Be a leader? Make money? Get promoted at your current job or land a better one? Be a live-entertainment entrepreneur? It's all possible. In fact, somebody's going to do all of that.

Why shouldn't it be you?

PART 1

WHY

PREAMBLE: THE LION WHO THOUGHT HE WAS A SHEEP

There was a lion that grew up in a flock of sheep and so he had no consciousness that he was a lion. He didn't know he was a lion. He would bleat like a sheep, he'd eat grass like a sheep. One day they were wandering at the edge of a big jungle when a mighty lion let out a big roar and leaped out of the forest and right into the middle of the flock. All the sheep scattered and ran away. Imagine the surprise of the jungle lion when he saw this other lion there among the sheep. So, he gave chase. He got hold of him. And there was this lion, cringing in front of the king of the jungle. And the jungle lion said to him, "What are you doing here?"

And the other lion said, "Have mercy on me. Don't eat me. Have mercy on me." But the king of the forest dragged him away saying "Come on with me." And he took him to a lake and he said, "Look." So, the lion who thought he was a sheep looked and for the first time he saw his reflection. He saw his image. Then he looked at the jungle lion, and he looked in the water again, and he let out a mighty roar. He was never a sheep again. It took only one minute.

—ANTHONY DEMELLO, *AWARENESS*

I love this story for so many reasons. It's cute. It's funny. But DeMello, one of the world's greatest storytellers, had a reason for telling this story. He told it for decades because it's more than a metaphor. The same pattern plays out in real life. All the time, in fact, and not just to individual people but entire groups.

Groups like the live entertainment industry.

We've convinced ourselves that we are sheep when in fact we are lions. The work we do, the skills we have, the mountains we move, the people we touch—all of it is the work of lions. It takes so much expertise, artistry, and care to do what we do. And it's all on full display, in real time, for all our paying customers to see. It could be a cozy cabaret, a giant stadium, or anything in between. It's near miraculous to create, sell, and produce these shows.

This is the work of lions.

How do we know this? People tell us with their wallets. They grumble when the cost of their Netflix subscription goes up a couple bucks a month, but they'll shell out many times that cost for a single night at a live event. We're at the top of the value pyramid, and people understand how great the product is.

But even though the product is great, even though people love and pay for what we do, we still cap our expectations.

Why? Because traditional live entertainment can only reach so many people at a time. Buildings have fire codes and fixed capacities. Seeing *Hamilton* may be the highlight of your year. It may be life-changing, but only 1,318 other people are going to see it with you that night.

Does *Hamilton* deserve only an audience of 1,319? Hell no. What does it deserve? A global audience of millions, that's what. Does the greatest band in Nashville deserve an audience of only a few thousand at a local venue? Of course not. It deserves an audience of people all over the world.

Nobody's a bigger fan of live events than me. All I need is a bag of peanut M&M's and a sippy cup of wine, and I'll watch anything on Broadway. Give me a beer and put me near the stage, and I'll rock all night. I've spent the last 20 years sending people to shows partly because it gets me closer to the shows.

I've seen so many great shows, some of them again and again. I remember a really powerful and strange theatre experience in downtown LA years ago. Afterward, I kept thinking about the people who'd want to see it and wishing they could. But of course, most of them couldn't. The show was a hit and sold out every night, but then it ended. If you weren't there on one of the nights it ran, it didn't exist for you.

I'll admit, there's something special about that smallness, the intimacy. Even in a 20,000-person arena, you're there with 19,999 other people and nobody else! The sense that *we* are here and they (everybody else) aren't has a certain power.

But...

It's time to ask if it has to be that way and whether or not that's what's important. Is exclusivity the only value we offer? Is the power of live, in-person entertainment the fact that a bunch of people get left out? I don't think so.

The power of the live event is being "there" for something special. It's bearing witness and celebrating with the rest of the faithful. It's not about who's left out. It's about who's there, and the more, the merrier.

Online events hold up a mirror to the live-entertainment community. Like the lion, if we look into that reflection, we'll see something mighty. We'll see an industry full of miracle workers. This is a group that delivers the product at the premium tip-top of the entertainment pyramid. The live experience towers above free music streaming, paid downloads, monthly subscriptions, and trips to the movie theatre.

People pay more for a live experience despite the inconvenience. They do it because it's special. It's different from everything else.

And you make these special moments possible.

For this, you deserve top-billing. And online events can get you there. They offer a viable path to new levels of success and opportunity.

The opportunity is too big to miss. And it's right in front of us.

I'm here to lay out the steps for success in this new world of online events. The first step is to simply see reality, perhaps for the first time. It's time to wake up from the dream that you're a sheep.

You're a lion.

CHAPTER 1

SCALE

In July of 2020, I filmed a series of videos about online events at the Pasadena Playhouse in Pasadena, California. A crew of three and I, socially distanced, Covid-tested, spent the whole day inside the beautiful, old building. We shot some videos explaining the importance of online events for live-entertainment creators.

Being there stirred up some strange, mixed feelings. I love the place. I've been there dozens of times and seen great work. And before me, for more than a century, thousands of others had come too. Right there. In the room, now silent and pandemic-empty, right there where we were.

At one point in the day, we took a break, and I did something the others probably found a little odd. I walked up and down the rows, my hand grazing over the top of each seat as I went. I walked through every row of the orchestra and then went up to the mezzanine and did the same. Six hundred and eighty-six seats. Six hundred and eighty-six places where a human being could sit and watch a show. Six hundred and eighty-six multiplied by a century.

HUMAN SCALE

It's not hard to picture 686 people. You could recognize that many people, learn their names, know something about each one of them. One of the most beautiful things about in-person, live events is that **human scale**. The sense that there's a finite group of people here. I could walk around the room and shake hands or say hello or play rock-paper-scissors with every single one of them.

People who work in live entertainment tend to appreciate this. Most of us have an empathy for the patrons who walk through our doors. Empathy makes it easier to do the job well, but it also tells you what kind of people choose this business. We're people people. Sorta. Kinda. Up to a point. If you don't get at least a little joy out of seeing a crowd of people having fun at a show, you might want to look for another job.

But there's a B-side to this. A downside, to be truthful. When you're too in love with human scale, you forget about global scale. Internet scale. What people in the tech business simply call "scale." To be in this business is to spend a lot of time thinking in hundreds or thousands and every now and then tens of thousands. Do that long enough and you might forget that numbers actually go higher. Much, much higher.

The legendary sci-fi writer Douglas Adams once wrote, "Space is big. Really big. You just won't believe how vastly hugely mind-bogglingly **big** it is. I mean you may think it's a long way down the road to the chemist [drug store], but that's just peanuts to space."[1]

You may think that selling out your 686-seat theatre or your 9,525-seat amphitheater (Red Rocks) or your 20,789-seat arena (Madison Square Garden) or your 65,618-seat stadium (Raymond

---

1   Douglas Adams, *The Hitchhiker's Guide to the Galaxy* (London: Picador, 2002), 66.

James Stadium) is big, but that's just peanuts compared to scale.

Take for example NBC's "live" production of *Grease* back in 2016. It was a modest (seriously, modest) success on television. Nearly 12.2 million people tuned in.[2] You could sniff at that number a little bit. It's not exactly Seinfeld-finale level, but here's another number for comparison: 13.3 million.

That's the number of *all* the people who went to *all* the shows on Broadway that same season.[3] It's not a fair comparison, I realize. People didn't have to brave midtown traffic or stand in line on 47th Street and have their bags checked for weapons to see the NBC production. I know, I know. It's not the same.

But brush away your initial impulse to dismiss this and simply consider what the numbers show. A decent production of a great, but tired, old show. A legacy network on a Sunday night. And it still had a bigger audience than all of Broadway for an entire year. Think about that again because it gives us a hint into the meaning of scale.

Big audiences, global reach, and internet speeds.

IT ALL STARTS WITH NUMBERS

I like to imagine the invention of numbers. Picture one of our distant ancestors somewhere on the savannah. She's trying to tell her tribemates that she has spotted some tasty-looking gazelles. She says, "Gazelle!" and now, she's got their attention. Two of the tribe saunter over with their stone-tipped spears. "No!" she says, struggling to express what's on her mind. "More!"

----

2   Wikipedia, s.v. "Grease: Live," last modified January 20, 2022, https://en.wikipedia.org/wiki/Grease:_Live#:~:text=Grease%3A%20Live%20was%20seen%20by,watched%20program%20of%20the%20night.

3   "2016–2017 Broadway End-of-Season Statistics," The Broadway League, May 23, 2017, https://www.broadwayleague.com/press/press-releases/2016-2017-broadway-end-of-season-statistics/.

They stare at her dumbly. They are the '80s-movie jocks of the Stone Age. She's broken their brains. She must find a way to get across the point that it's going to take more than this number of hunters to get this done.

She looks at her hand, on which are conveniently located several fingers. *Hmm.* She folds her thumb behind her hand, concealing it from the view of these lovable dummies.

"Four gazelle!" she says, coining the word "four" in her language. The idea blossoms in their minds: there are precisely "four" gazelles!

In the next few days, our heroine goes on to invent words for one, two, three, five, six, seven, eight, nine, and ten. Along with "four," these new words are a head-spinning leap in technology! It changes how the tribe thinks. I need *three* sticks to finish this shelter. I want to eat *two* giant slabs of meat. Let's fill *five* baskets with these tasty plants before we go back home.

She stops at 10 because she's never had to talk about 11 of anything. She's seen 11 (and more) of a lot of things, but communicating the idea of 11 of something hasn't come up. So she creates a word that roughly translates as "a lot" and concludes the project. Why create a number bigger than 10? When would that ever come up? Besides, you're out of fingers.

Time goes on and the numbers one through 10 serve them well, but nobody in the tribe happens to invent any others. Over time, the numbers serve the tribe well, but they also create a sort of ceiling on their imaginations. *The numbers in their heads make them what they are.* As time goes on, their brains form themselves around the numbers they use.

And that's fine for a long, long time. But across the valley, there's a tribe that competes with them for food and other resources. The tribes used to be about the same size, but the other tribe now seems bigger. This year, it's going to be dryer than usual, and gazelle might be scarcer. That means it's uncertain whether two tribes can thrive in the same valley. One morning, precisely 124 members of the other tribe come calling. They've got some pretty specific thoughts about this drought situation.

Someone over there invented bigger numbers, and they've been using them.

The numbers in our heads make us what we are as an industry too. We give high-fives to our team when we bring in events that sell 1,000 tickets on day one. And rightly so! It's difficult to create or market an event that catches on with an audience willing to come physically to a venue and spend good money for the privilege.

That doesn't change the reality that in a world with seven or eight billion people in it, 1,000 is a small number. It's perfectly fine to have a small audience. A great show or work of art or performance can have a life-changing impact, even if it's only on a few people. Nothing's wrong with having a small audience.

Unless you want a larger audience.

THINKING BIGGER

Do you want a larger audience? Most people I know in the live events industry do. That's why they do marketing. They create social media content. They make phone calls. They run ads. They create event artwork that maximizes the appeal of what they're selling. Their organizations and artists work with companies like Goldstar to reach new people. There's an understandable thirst for growing and cultivating a bigger audience.

Financially, size makes a big difference, and we'll see why in the next chapter. But there's something else too. It's natural and good to want more people to see what you've got coming to your stage. If you've got an audience of 100, it's good to want your audience to be 200. If you've got an audience of 200, it's good to want your audience to be 500. If you've got an audience of 10,000, it's good to want your audience to be 50,000.

It's good to want your audience to be bigger. In fact, it's good to want your audience to be *way* bigger. Tens of thousands more. Millions more. Billions more? Don't rule it out.

Most marketers in live entertainment think in smallish numbers because that's what they've had until now. They think, *If I could get 10 percent more people to show up, wouldn't that be great?*

If you find yourself thinking that thought, I want to suggest a replacement. Instead of dreaming about 10 percent more people in your audience, think this instead: *I want everybody to be in our audience.*

You might not get everybody, but why not start there and work your way down? After all, we've done the opposite for long enough.

It's good to want everybody to be in your audience.

This is important for two reasons. First, when you think small, you put an instant limit on yourself. To be fair, venues actually do have limits. Even Wembley Stadium or the Rose Bowl only holds so many. If you can't seat a million, why worry about having a million customers?

Which is where the second reason comes in: it's now possible to accommodate way more people than can physically fit in your venue. With online event technologies, having everybody in your audience is actually *possible.*

Even if you don't get a billion, your ambitions are no longer limited by the number of dates and seats. Those constraints are gone.

The only constraint left is learning to get the most out of these new technologies. Yes, you'll have to create the right content and reinvent the marketing formula. But before you can do that, you'll have to remove the limits on your own thinking.

I'm like Carl Sagan staring into the camera and talking about the "billions and billions of stars" in the universe. He stood on a beach and grabbed a handful of sand. Looking into the camera, he said, "The Cosmos is rich beyond measure: the total number of stars in the universe is greater than all the grains of sand on all the beaches of the planet Earth."[4]

In the same way, the world is rich beyond measure with potential fans for the work that you're creating. Maybe not more than all the grains of sand, but still a lot more than you can reach now.

Let's do a little thought experiment to see how big your audience should be. Don't worry too much about getting these numbers right. The experiment is meant to illustrate a general idea.

Start by estimating what percentage of people *might* be interested in your shows. Your work may have a broad appeal, like big, old-fashioned musicals or pop music. It might be more of a niche, like Mongolian throat singing or long-form performance art. That's fine. Estimate how many people out of 100 entertainment-buying adults *might* be interested in what you do. Not how many already attend your events, but how many might want to, under the right circumstances.

Got your number out of 100? Great. Let's say it's 8 percent. That makes it a specialized taste, not a fluffy rom-com or Dolly Parton. But as you'll see, that's okay. Because 8 percent of the reachable population of the world is more than 100 million people! You won't get them all, of course. But every one of these people in the global middle-class has access and money.

One hundred million people! Would that do?

- - - - - - - - - - -

4   Carl Sagan, *Cosmos* (New York: Ballantine Books, 1985), 161.

Next question: how many people do you *actually* serve? I'm going to go out on a limb and say it's *not* 100 million.

Fair enough. With only in-person events, reaching your *true* audience would be impossible. But things have changed.

Now, 100 million people are waiting for you. Can you picture them?

When you see the numbers in a new way, you see the world in a new way. In that new world, your opportunities start looking pretty cosmic.

PICTURING YOUR AUDIENCE

I keep thinking about Carl Sagan and his handful of beach sand. He said the number of grains of sand equaled the approximate number of stars we can see with the naked eye. That's about 10,000 stars.

I tried to find a way to picture audiences at scale, so I spent a couple hours on the exercise I'm about to describe. Here's how you can play along.

First, get a box of paper clips or anything small and numerous. Thumb tacks, those little mint chocolates, marbles. It doesn't matter, but get a big box of them. I used paper clips.

Pick up one paper clip and imagine it represents 100 people at a show. Take a look at the paper clip and really try to imagine 100 people. Picture how many rows they take up, how long it takes to scan them in at the door. See their faces. Imagine how much noise they make. Everything. Now place that paper clip on a table or desk, and you have ticketed and seated that group. Feels good, right?

Now pick up six more. Add four to the first row to complete a row of five. Then start another row right below that one with the two you have left. Now you've got a row of five and two more in an incomplete row below it. That's seven paper clips, or 700 people.

You've now filled the Official State Theatre of California, the Pasadena Playhouse, in beautiful Pasadena, California.

Cool, right? But we're not done. Below that original set of seven paper clips, lay down another set in the same way. Now you've got 1,400 people. Take a second and think about a group that size. You've seen groups like this many times, but it's a lot more than the 100 people we pictured at the beginning.

Now, do this 26 more times. In other words, 28 sets of seven paper clips. Go on, actually do it. It took me 10 or 15 minutes, in no small part because I kept getting bored. But press on!

Stand up and take a step back because now you're looking at nearly 20,000 people. This is a major crowd. If you work at the Staples Center, you see crowds about this size every night. Go back and remember how it looked and felt at each stage. Picture the first 100 people, then the 700 who filled the theatre, and now the 20,000 filling an arena.

When I reached this point, I had covered half my desk in paper clips. I could feel the sheer immensity of the numbers I was looking at.

And it was only 20,000.

I thought about pressing on to 100,000, but I didn't have enough paper clips or desk space. And I didn't want to spend two more hours putting down paper clips.

In theory, I could put out paper clips representing 1,000,000 people, but that would have taken me all night. And the paper clips would have covered the floor of my office.

Still, you can picture a floor covered with paper clips to represent an audience of 1,000,000. This might seem like an unreachable number, but it happened during an online concert in October of

2020. The K-pop band BTS drew 993,000 paying fans for one event.[5] There's your 1,000,000-person audience, your floor covered with paper clips.

In live entertainment, we look at those finite rooms full of people and appreciate them. We care about them, obsess over the experience they're going to have. Those first few "paper clips" really are special and important. But it's also important that our minds are open to all those other people as well. We have to be able to think in our smallish numbers to keep the live, in-person experience special. But we also have to add zeros to our thinking. We have to be able to picture 1,000,000 people logging on and watching as easily as we can picture a few thousand walking through a turnstile.

In other words, it's important that we can think in scale.

The next chapter will address why it's so important that we think this way. The live business model makes financial success hard. Scale-thinking and online event technology can change that.

---

5   "BTS'Map of the Soul ON:E' draws 993,000 viewers," Rappler.com, October 13, 2020, https://www.rappler.com/entertainment/music/viewers-bts-online-concert-october-2020.

100 People

Pasadena Playhouse
(~700 People)

Staples Center
(~28 Pasadena Playhouses)

BTS Online Concert Oct. 2020
(~50 Staples Centers)

CHAPTER 2

BUSINESS MODEL OF
THE DAMNED

If you've ever produced a live show, you've got something in common with everyone else who has.

Throughout the run of that show, possibly to an obsessive level, there was a number in your head.

Your break-even.

Whether you think in dollars, tickets, or percent of house, this number is the key. You have to know how close you are to it, if it's changed, and if you're ahead of it.

This number is vital, especially if it's your money or job on the line. The financial goal of most shows is not to break even. It's to make money, even if you're a totally mission-driven nonprofit. The bottom line matters for everyone.

And reaching the right number isn't exactly easy. For most in-person, live-entertainment events, you break even around 65 percent sold out. Your results may vary, but it's rarely 50 percent or 80 percent.[6]

----

6 Common exceptions to this are productions that either have outside funding making them possible or whose goal is to make money in future productions. Often, the most elaborate,

Of course, once you hit break-even for a single show, it starts all over again, possibly for the next night. In many other businesses, you hit break-even, and that holds you for quite a while.

Let's say you're manufacturing toasters. You have startup costs and other costs to get your fine, new toaster on the market. Toasters have a break-event point too, but there's one very important difference.

When you hit toaster break-even, you don't have to start again the next day. You might hit break-even on toasters and then make money for months or years! This is The Good Place! Profitability. With a ticketed show, though, the count starts over with every show. You go back to The Bad Place (before you hit break-even) and have to climb your way out again.

PROFIT AND LOSS

The difference is in the structure of the industry. It's the very nature of the business. I call it the *Business Model of the Damned.*

I'm being dramatic, but it feels that way sometimes, and there's a reason. Live entertainment is a business with *high fixed costs* and *low variable costs.* That means it costs a lot just to put on a show, regardless of what happens after you make the decision to produce one. Renting a facility, paying talent, constructing sets and lighting, paying the union technicians, hiring security—you pay for all of it *regardless of how many tickets you sell.* Some of it will go up a little bit or down a little bit in response to how well a show does, but

---

expensive operas are paid for by a donation or campaign, and sometimes, pre-Broadway runs of a new theatre production are not aiming to make money on the preliminary run, but on later runs on Broadway or touring. In these cases, breaking even is literally not mathematically possible given capacity and pricing.

not much. Once you say "Go!" to putting on a show, your costs don't change much.

In the restaurant business, by contrast, costs drop if customers don't show up. Food accounts for 30 to 40 percent of the cost to serve a restaurant patron. If fewer patrons show up, less food is used, and what's left unused can often be used later. Labor needs in a restaurant go up and down too. Labor also represents 30 to 40 percent of costs, and if a restaurant's business slows down, labor costs can go down. I used to work in the restaurant business. If things got particularly slow, I'd ask for volunteers to clock out early and hold the last few baking runs of the day. Voila! I've turned a losing day into an alright(ish) day.

That's hard to do in live entertainment. You can't tell half the cast to stay home. Or try to get a reduction on the equipment rentals for the night because sales weren't great. It just doesn't work that way.

Not every industry has this same structure, with high fixed and low variable costs. But in-person, live events do, and that's why we live or die by the break-even. In a business with lower fixed costs, you can adjust. You can actually move your break-even point down *on the fly* if you need to.

We're not alone. Other industries have this same structure, so much so that you can picture it. Imagine an airline scheduling a flight from Chicago to Atlanta. What have you got? You've got high fixed costs—flying a giant metal tube through the sky at 500 miles per hour ain't cheap—and low variable costs. Each individual customer gets about two minutes of staff attention, a bag of peanuts, and a coke.

Let's talk about those low variable costs. Once the door to that plane closes, so do the books. The financial outcome is now certain. But what if a Chicago businesswoman needs to take a last-minute trip to visit her clients at Coca-Cola in Atlanta? She walks up to the ticket counter just in time to get herself on the plane. She spends $1,000 for her ticket and runs through the airport, arriving at the gate with seconds to spare.

If you're the airline, you get the whole $1,000. Did you spend any more money? Not much, if any. The gate personnel's salary hasn't changed. You're out a bag of peanuts and a soda, but really, you've spent next to nothing while collecting the fare. The whole $1,000 goes to the bottom line. Boom! That flight is much more profitable than it was before.

You see the similarity. That same businesswoman learns that Justin Bieber, her secret guilty musical pleasure, is playing at State Farm Arena. She rushes out of her last meeting, arrives at the box office five minutes before the show starts, and buys a ticket. What happens?

Same thing as our airplane example. Her $150 goes into the coffers with almost no costs to serve her.[7]

And when the metaphorical doors of the concert close, that's it. Just like on an airplane.

THE JOURNEY TOWARD THE GOOD PLACE

Selling a live-entertainment show is like going on a journey. This journey goes through The Bad Place and, if you're lucky, arrives at The Good Place. In The Bad Place, you're losing money on the show. In The Good Place, you're making money, but because of the structure we just talked about, there's a twist. And since this is the Business Model of the Damned, it's not a fun twist. It's more of a *Twilight Zone*–style twist.

---

7   Not strictly true because of things like ticketing-software fees paid by the venue in some cases, but the point remains.

In the graph below, you can see how this works. The dotted line represents your costs, which are pretty much fixed, and so the line is flat. When you sell ticket one, your revenues, on the left of the graph, go up. The gap between your sales and your expenses is still big, of course, but that's okay for now. As you sell more, the gap closes, but until you get to break-even, you're still in The Bad Place.

You'll notice it takes an awfully long time to get out of there, and of course, many shows never do. But let's not dwell on that. We're shooting for the moon on our example show! Push through break-even, and you're now in The Good Place! Hallelujah!

The good thing about The Good Place is that it gets Gooder and Gooder faster and faster. At break-even plus $1, your total profit is $1. That's better than losing money, but it's not much. As you keep going, your profit begins a rapid path up! You work like crazy to sell to get to break-even, but if you keep going another 5 percent, you're making okay money! Another 5 percent after that, and you've doubled your profits for just having sold 5 percent more! It's amazing! That's why we call it The Good Place.

So you're flying along, selling everything. Money is raining from the sky like actual rain. You get to 80, 85, and then 90 percent sold, and you're thinking of buying a pair of shoes dipped in gold. You hit 95 percent, and now you're down to the scattered handful of unsold seats. But people don't care! They buy those tickets too, and you sell out!

And now the twist. That beautiful ride you were on is over! That slamming sound you heard was you hitting The Wall. Just when things were getting Good. Just when you couldn't miss with sales, and every ticket you sold was making you real, bottom-line money, you hit The Wall, otherwise known as *capacity*.

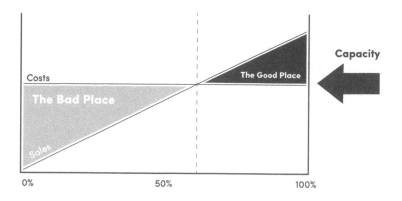

Is this some kind of joke? Just when you've got the formula right, just when it's all going your way, Game Over. Thanks for playing.

Imagine if Apple built the world's greatest smartphone, produced a bunch, sold out of them, and had to call it quits. "We sold all the phones we made. Sorry. Maybe we'll make something else later."

Crazy, right? But that's our business because of the physical limits of capacity. And because The Wall doesn't care about your feelings or your profit-and-loss statement (P&L).

That's the industry we're in, and it works. More or less. The appeal of our product is high, and we can charge a lot for it because people like live shows. Still, there's a sword-dangling-over-your-head quality to working in this industry most of the time. And the more your job or wallet relies on sales, the more precarious that sword looks.

Of course, you're not completely without options if you want to extend your time in The Good Place. You can squeeze a few more tickets out by opening previously unavailable seating options. Every venue has some barely acceptable chairs stored somewhere in the venue. You can always use those in a pinch. I've sat in chairs that, I feel quite sure, came out of conference rooms but were doubling as over-overflow seats. Talk about a "house seat"!

The other option is to extend. Let me revise that: the other option is that you can *sometimes* extend for a limited period. I remember several years ago, Lady Gaga and Tony Bennett had a mini tour that was just on fire in a few locations. The belief was that demand would be solid but not off the charts. So some of the larger venues closed the bigger, further-back sections. Demand at one famous outdoor venue, however, was just epic. They opened the sections of a previously closed "balcony" for two of the scheduled dates, but that wasn't enough. In the end, two more dates were added, and demand was ultimately filled.

But think about that. To fill the demand, two more dates had to be put on the calendar. Two more trips through The Bad Place to get Good. The marketing team on this show had to agonize about the decision because the *fixed cost* of adding those dates was certain and significant. And demand, though strong, is uncertain and eventually runs out.

It was a successful run, but the last two dates didn't quite sell out. Adding them was net profitable, but that was fortunate. Had demand not panned out quite as well, it's conceivable this runaway hit could have ended up a money loser. Defeat seized from the jaws of victory. Again, I call it the Business Model of the Damned for a reason.

Shifting the Business Model

Online events can help tilt the board more in our favor. In the short history of online events, organizations have used this new medium to do previously impossible things. Remember the example of BTS? In the summer of 2019, BTS played three sold-out dates at the Rose Bowl in Pasadena, each date with a capacity of over 80,000. Impressive, right? For days, BTS fans swarmed Pasadena, carrying signs and wearing their merch. It felt like everyone in the world had come to town to see the show.

But it was less than a quarter of the number who would see them in just one online show in October 2020. That online show created the revenue and audience equivalent of an entire tour. In 90 minutes.

How does this change the business model? With online events, The Good Place becomes the New and Improved Good Place. It's improved because it just keeps going. With no capacity limits, a successful show can become very successful indeed. When you've caught lightning in a bottle with a good show, you can keep going. You don't have to duplicate your whole cost structure again by offering a new date. Because there's no capacity limit, there's no Wall to stop the fun. Once you've exited The Bad Place, you can stay in The Good Place as long as you can keep selling.

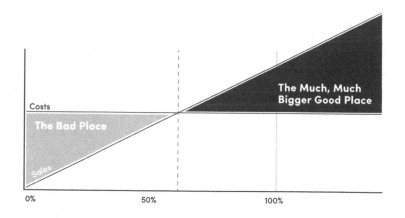

This is true for both pure online events and hybrid events (we'll cover the pluses and minuses of both in a later chapter). Here's what to remember for now: the lack of a capacity limit means profitability on a show can get absolutely crazy.

Let's take a simplified, but still realistic, example.

Let's imagine you have a show with fixed costs of $600,000. You plan to sell tickets at $30 each. Ignoring some details to keep things simple, that makes your break-even 20,000 tickets sold.

In a physical venue, that would usually require about 65 to 70 percent of your capacity. Let's say it's exactly two-thirds of it (66.6 percent), so your gross potential on the show is right at $900,000 and 30,000 tickets.

In that case, here's your profitability as you go from ticket one to sold out: At 65 percent, you've come a long way. It's not easy to sell nearly 20,000 tickets, but you're still losing about $15,000. Ah, but at 70 percent, you're now up $30,000! That feels good. From a small loss to a small profit.

But 80 percent feels a lot better because that nice, tidy $30,000 has turned into $120,000. With just 3,000 more tickets sold, you've increased your profits by more than three times. From a small profit to a nice, chunky one.

At 90 percent, you're up to $210,000 in profit on this show. Everybody's going to be happy about this. You might even have raised prices and started to think about adding more dates by now.

At 100 percent sold, the profitability on your show is over $300,000. That's the good news. The bad news is you've hit The Wall. You could add a date, but then you're starting this whole thing over again. You could quit, but how often do you have something this hot, where every dollar that comes in is pure gravy?

If this were an online show, you wouldn't have to stop at all. If you've got sales momentum, you could add another 10, 20, 50, or 100 percent. Whatever the demand for the show may be, you can add it. Selling up to 125 percent of your original capacity takes your profits to over half a million dollars!

We'll talk in depth about hybrid events later, but here's something to activate your thinking. If you add an online component to an in-person event, and it adds just 20 percent to revenue, it adds a lot more to profits.

For example, suppose sales for your in-person event bog down at 60 percent. It happens, right? But in this case, if it does, you're in a position to lose $60,000. If the online event also generates revenue, even at a much lower rate, it could make a big difference. Let's imagine that in this case, it adds another 10 percent to the total sold. Without the online event, you were losing $60,000, but now, you've nearly broken even, losing just a few thousand dollars, a gap you can make up.[8] If your online event had done better, adding, say, 20 percent, your disappointing show would have netted $48,000. Everyone goes home happy. Or at least less disappointed and out of pocket.

And that's for a show that *isn't* successful. You can imagine the impact as you keep going up.

LOVE WHAT YOU DO AND MAKE MONEY

Most of us in the live entertainment industry love what we do. What's on our stages isn't just some neutral "product." We're not selling oven mitts or renter's insurance. We care about the music or the play or the comedy routine. We know the performers and even watch them build their careers. We talk about the shows outside of work just for fun.

Not only that, but we care about the fans and ticket holders too. We know what they need and like (and what they don't like), and we

- - - - - - - - - - - -

8   Hybrid events are in-person events that are also made available as an online event. The costs of producing an online event on top of an in-person event are small enough that for a large event, they'll be negligible.

want to give it to them. We may sometimes get a little salty about it at the end of a long day, but it doesn't mean we don't care. It means making a great show happen takes a lot out of us. Demands come from every direction, and there is a lot that has to go right. But it somehow always does. I credit that to a group of highly skilled people who care enough to make good and sure that it all works.

But nothing's perfect. We have great people, but as we've seen, we have a business model with a major flaw in it. We have to work extremely hard just to break even. And once we do, we've got a narrow profit window before the fun comes to an end and the show reaches capacity.

With online events, we can take an underperforming event and turn it into a big profit-driver. And sometimes, one online event might do what entire tours do over the course of months. Just ask BTS.

If you're thinking, "Yeah, but I'm not BTS," you're right.[9] Very few acts, artists, or venues can generate $45 million in a single online show. Chances are, whoever you are, you probably can't either.

But I'm also willing to bet that you don't need $45 million to make a big impact on you, your artist, or your organization. It wouldn't take rock-star Rolls-Royce-in-a-swimming-pool money to get your attention, would it?

And if the financial potential of online events doesn't excite you, there's more. Even if you have plenty of money, or just don't care about money, there's something I bet you do care about: people, reach, supporters, patrons, fans. Whatever you call them, I know you want them.

In the next chapter, we'll talk about how online events help you get them.

----

9   Unless you are BTS, in which case, #btsarmy! Call me to arrange your next online show.

_ _ _ _

CHAPTER 3

THE AUDIENCE YOU DESERVE

At this point, you might have the wrong impression of me. I've focused a lot on numbers and money, and you might picture me at my desk in a green eyeshade surrounded by stacks of gold coins.

I wish! Not for the green eyeshade, but certainly I'd take the gold coins.

Still, you might be thinking I see this business only through the lens of money and numbers. Not at all. Like everyone I know who has spent years in the industry, I care about the shows, the music, the work. I love it! I can't wait to see what's touring this summer or what's coming to Broadway. I love stumbling into a little venue and having an amazing, unexpected night of fun.

If I were selling oven mitts or renter's insurance, I'd go crazy. I mention this because if you're reading this, you're probably the same.

There's another reason to get good at online events. If you love the work, you want more people to see and enjoy it. Don't you agree?

Years ago, I saw an immersive play called *Alma* in a beautiful-but-crumbling old movie theater in downtown LA. It was one of the greatest entertainment experiences of my life. To this day, it's the only show I've been to that included an actual bus ride through the neighborhood. I loved it, and I wasn't alone. The show was a hit! It got a multi-week extension, which was also popular, but then... it ended. I calculate that as many as a couple thousand people saw the show, but thousands more, at least, *should* have seen it.

And I've thought the same thing many times since about other events I've experienced in a live venue. Can you relate?

But the hard reality is that despite what these experiences *deserve*, they only get what they get. That's unfortunate, not just for the people producing the show, but for all the people who don't get to see it.

Here's a hypothetical example that's haunted me since I thought of it.

Imagine the world's greatest small theatre organization. This is a group of people that produces the absolute best theatrical work in a venue under, say, 250 seats. There are thousands of these groups out there. Hundreds in places like New York and Los Angeles. Dozens in small cities like Seattle and Denver.

Imagine the very best one; the one delivering the greatest, most interesting work.

Whoever they are, you'll agree they're doing some awesome work. Even if you're not a theatre fan, you can appreciate that the best in a field of thousands has got to be pretty darn good.

I ask myself, how big of an audience does this organization *deserve*? "Deserve" is a tricky word, of course. Some would argue that you get what you deserve by definition. I take the point, but let's broaden the definition just enough to say that good work deserves a bigger audience than less-good work. Let's agree that merit isn't the only factor in popularity. Sometimes, the best stuff stays obscure because of circumstances or luck.

Given that, now what do you think? How big of an audience does the World's Greatest Small Theatre Organization deserve?

Assume there are hundreds of millions of theatre fans around the world. There could be a billion or more, if you count casual fans.

Ten percent of a billion is 100 million people. Does an organization like this deserve to have 10 percent of all theatre fans know its work? I think it does.

Perhaps you disagree. Ten percent is too big, you say? Okay, how about 1 percent? That's 10 million people. You're going to have a hard time arguing me down from that number very much. Why wouldn't 1 percent of theatre fans want to see the world's greatest small theatre? The number should be much higher, but fine. Let's assume 1 percent of theatre fans are interested.

Ten million people it is, then. Cool. That's a good number of people, a serious fandom.

But let's compare that number to reality. If this organization is a 250-seat theatre and sells out the typical 200 performances a year, 50,000 people see their work. For a small theatre, this is not bad. If you're part of a small theater, you might even be drooling at this number.

But we just said that even a very trimmed down potential audience for this is more like 10 million. That's 200 times *more* people than the actual, current audience. It's as if there are 200 seats in the theatre and only one person showed up.

Or look at it this way. Do you think the world's greatest small theatre deserves a bigger audience than the lowest-rated sitcom on television? Because if you do, then 10 million people is *low* for that show.

FANDOM AND PEAK EXPERIENCES

Let's talk about "audience" for a second. The terms we use sometimes sound a little dated. "Patron," for example, sounds like somebody who pays da Vinci to paint a mural. "Customers" sound like people in line for a haircut, and "ticket buyers"...well, this is an obvious dud.

You hear a lot of talk today about fandoms. It's a mash-up implying a "kingdom" of "fans." Like the word "Christendom," it implies that the artist or organization rules a vast territory. Sports teams often talk about their "nations." "Red Sox Nation" or "Lakers Nation," for example, are the people, wherever they are, who support that team.

In live entertainment, the notion of fandom needs to come more to the forefront. In early 2020, Bruce Campbell assembled his fandom. Bruce is the star of the *Evil Dead* series of movies from the '80s and early '90s. Director Sam Raimi, Bruce, and Joel Cohen (of Cohen brothers fame) made the first *Evil Dead* movie on a shoestring budget. For reasons some might find inexplicable, it became an enduring classic that spawned two higher-budget sequels, which comprise the original trilogy. Successful at the box office and on VHS, *Evil Dead* is a wacked-out take on the zombie/ ghost/horror genre. Bruce, as the main character, Ash, is the only thing standing between our world and unspeakable evil.

Generations of people have watched and enjoyed the *Evil Dead* movies, and so there's a fandom. They show up at "cons," connect online, and gobble up new adaptations, including video games, comic books, a television series that ran for three seasons from 2015 to 2018, and even a live musical. They are *Evil Dead* Nation.

Bruce Campbell could walk down a busy street and go unrecognized, but to his fandom, he's a huge star. He matters.

In January of 2021, Bruce gave his fans the opportunity during the pandemic to watch the first *Evil Dead* movie with him online.

The premise was very simple: Bruce watched the movie while telling stories and jokes and being charming, all broadcasted on the internet. He chatted with and answered questions from the online audience in front of a green screen.

Thousands of people paid an average of $35 to join in, and they had a great time. The chat was friendly, funny, and constant. The hand-clap and zombie emojis flew across the screen the whole time. Bruce answered questions and delighted dozens of fans with direct, personal answers. It was a love fest.

His fandom showed up for him because he gave them a way to do so. And because he created a way for his fandom to gather, it grew.

Taking this example, we see that online events are a way to both *bring together* and *build* a fandom. Of course, in-person events do this too, but they're limited by distance and capacity. Bruce Campbell also tours, doing a similar show in person, and this doesn't stop because of online events. Banish that "either/or" thinking right now.

An online event removes the limitations of place for the fandom. You can reach fans where they are without hauling all that gear around the country. Even more, online events *create* a place that feels real and exists only to gather your group. It's no fun being a fan of something all by yourself, and online events bring people together to have a blast.

A live event is an intense experience! It's part of why people pay good money to go. You're together in one "place" with a bunch of other people, and your minds and spirits meld. The experience you're sharing creates a powerful bond. This is even truer for people with something already in common. Fans of the same sports team, for example, have a quasi-religious kind of experience at a game. They're cheering for their color and cursing the other guys. They're doing something together, a collective action, and it's all-consuming.

Online events are special because they bring people together and give them a peak experience from the comfort of wherever they happen to be, requiring no travel, physical interaction, or dress code. If you can offer this special experience, people will be willing—no, happy—to pay you for it.

GATHER YOUR TRIBE AND EXPAND YOUR REACH

In December of 2020, the cast of the musical *Jagged Little Pill* (*JLP*) reunited under strict safety protocols to do a concert version of the music from the show. *JLP* had a big fandom despite only having run on Broadway for a few months before the shutdown. The Alanis Morrisette album of the same name had been earning fans for decades. The show struck a chord with audiences, and people wanted to see more!

On December 13th, 20,000 people paid an average of $30 to watch *Jagged Live in NYC: A* Broadway Reunion Concert on Stellar. The cast performed live from a theatre in midtown Manhattan, and their fans loved it. You could tell because the in-show chat was nonstop, upbeat, and friendly. There were the usual cheers and song requests of course, but it was more than that. The *JLP* fans there that night weren't just shouting into a void. They were talking to *each other* as the show was going on. They were confirming their identity as fans of the music and the show. They got to meet others with the same interest and reunite with friends.

In other words, *JLP* gathered its tribe! By the time the show was over, the crowd was out of its mind with excitement for what they had just experienced. The cast knocked their performances out of the park, but it was more than that. It was the fact that the online event format brought the fandom together from literally all over the world—and people were constantly saying where they were watching from in the chat. The format gave everyone a shared experience.

Half an hour after the show was over, fans were still in the chat, talking and hanging out. It wasn't even so much about *JLP* anymore. It was about each other. Our own Stellar moderator even got a marriage proposal and a nomination for President in 2024. It was a fun and moving night for the *JLP* Nation.

But was that all it was? A fun night, some work for the cast, and some good money coming into the bank account? It certainly was all of that. It was also much more. *Jagged Live in NYC: A Broadway Reunion Concert* happened during the heart of the pandemic shutdown. "Gathering the tribe" in person was impossible at the time, forcing the online format.

But if you think about it, they did something they couldn't have done if Broadway was open. They brought people together from all over the world in a way that allowed them to connect. They had an audience ten times the size of their usual audience. People from dozens of countries were there, including many who'll never make it to New York.

Expanding *reach* has obvious benefits. In the entertainment business, capturing the imagination of people is what it's all about. A great show just isn't the same if nobody sees it.

Now more than ever, people express love (not just like) for their favorite art and entertainment. For its part, *JLP* engaged thousands of new people. It created a new customer list, an asset on which to build future success for the show. While most Broadway shows were licking their wounds and waiting, *JLP* brought people together.[10]

---

10 *Jagged Little Pill* closed on Broadway in December of 2021, amid the Omicron wave of live entertainment cancellations. However, it announced a nationwide tour in February of 2021.

NOT JUST A COVID STOPGAP

Even after the pandemic, online events will have special advantages. They will continue to offer spaces where people around the world can meet and have peak experiences together.

Some people see the limitations of space and capacity as good things. Scarcity, they believe, means that people really, really value what they see on a stage. If it were easier to get, they'd value it less, pay less, and lose interest.

Is this true? If so, we should be concerned.

Let's find out with a thought experiment. Travel back in time with me to the year 1984. Imagine you are the commissioner of the National Basketball Association (NBA). Don't worry. You don't have to be an expert about basketball or know much at all about it to play along here.[11]

It's 1984, and your league is on a roll. It wasn't always this way. In fact, there were some moments in the 1970s when it looked like the league might not make it at all. Things got really bad. A rival league innovated its way to success. In the end, the NBA had to absorb its rival's top teams and players and even copy some of its new rules. The three-point shot, for example, was added to the rulebook.

Even with that, interest was lukewarm. Believe it or not, the NBA Finals games weren't always broadcast live. As late as 1981, if you were watching the NBA championship, you were probably watching it on a tape delay.

Then something wonderful happened. Two guys named Magic Johnson and Larry Bird came into the league at the same time.

----

11 If you're not from North America or really, really don't know anything at all about professional basketball, imagine the biggest, most popular sports league where you are, and this example should still work.

They became the two best players in the league and formed a rivalry that was better and more exciting than anything before it. Interest in the game exploded. Basketball suddenly became cool in a whole new way. It even surpassed baseball in popularity and still had room to grow.

And now, in 1984, the gods have sent you yet another blessing: Michael Jordan. The rookie from the University of North Carolina brings talent and a style that's unlike anything that came before. The man can fly! Under your leadership (and with a little luck), the NBA has gone from near-death to business nirvana.

And in the midst of this, your VP of Marketing comes to you with a provocative proposal. He sees the rise in interest, the fans flocking to the arenas where before they were half-empty. He sees the jerseys with player names on them adorning the backs of school kids and young adults alike. He can feel the value of the NBA brand rising by the day, and he wants to make sure that continues.

His proposal: stop putting the games on TV. If fans can see professional basketball on TV, why would they come to the games? If they can flip a switch and get their NBA fix, they'll value it less. "It's basic supply and demand," he says. "If we create too much supply, the price people are willing to pay will drop. They won't value the true basketball experience, which is in the arena, if they can see it at home. They won't pay for tickets. They'll settle for the lesser but cheaper thing, and our business will stop growing."

Sound familiar? I've heard this same argument against online events for years now. Before the pandemic, times were pretty good for in-person events, so this rather weak argument held up. Or at least, it allowed people to ignore online events.

But that doesn't mean it makes any sense.

Back to our thought experiment. It's 1984, and you're the commissioner of the NBA. Your VP of Marketing proposes you stop putting basketball games on TV. You know TV expands your reach by hundreds or even thousands of times your reach in venues alone, but he seems to have a point. But is he right? That's the question.

If you accept the VP's proposal, flash forward to today. Is the NBA *more* or *less* successful? Is its fan base *bigger* or *smaller?* Do the players, coaches, staff, and owners do *better* or *worse* financially? Are there *more* or *fewer* fans and players of basketball around the world?

The answer is obvious of course. Making it possible for your product to *reach* as many people as possible is good. Giving them more and more ways to watch, join in, pay you, and enjoy being a fan is always the right decision. That's especially true when the product is as great as pro basketball.

Or as great as what you put on stage.

So now you know *why* you should be doing online events. In the next part of the book, we're going to dig into *how* to do these events and make them successful.

PART 2

HOW

PREAMBLE: PAY-PER-VIEW AND YOU

By now, you're convinced of the opportunity online events represent. The financial, artistic, and audience-building potential opens a new level of possibilities.

Now, your mind may be turning to questions about just how to put together a successful event, and that's what Part 2 is all about. Online events are new, and there's no shame in not already being an expert. That's what this book is for!

Though online events are new, the concept isn't. In a way, online events are an evolution of something quite old (and quite successful): pay-per-view.

Pay-per-view? Are you kidding? I know it sounds old-fashioned. I picture clicking the "buy" button on the clunky, old '90s cable remote when I hear "pay-per-view." I even remember the days of dialing a number and talking to a person to order a pay-per-view event.

Pay-per-view has been around for a while, since the 1950s in fact. In September 1981, Sugar Ray Leonard fought Thomas "Hitman" Hearns in a particularly popular pay-per-view event. Only one cable system offered it, but according to some sources, *more than half* of its customers bought it.[12]

Since then, of course, pay-per-view has taken a lot of forms and become quite lucrative. If you've ever seen one of those listicles online about the world's highest paid athletes, you probably recognize a lot of the names. Even if you don't follow sports, you might know LeBron James, Ronaldo, Lionel Messi, and Tiger Woods.

----

12 Wikipedia, s.v. "Pay-per-View," last modified January 23, 2022, https://en.wikipedia.org/wiki/Pay-per-view.

But near the top of recent lists is one name that may not be as well recognized in the United States. Even some sports fans don't know Canelo Álvarez. The fourth highest paid athlete in the world on the Forbes 2019 list, Álvarez made more than LeBron, Aaron Rodgers, and other big names that year.

Two things made Álvarez different from his neighbors in this elite neighborhood. First, he's a boxer, and second, unlike the rest of them, he only worked two nights in 2019. LeBron schlepped up and down the court for more than 100 games. Tiger Woods walked the golf course four days a week for most of the year. And Lionel Messi put in 90-plus solid minutes on the soccer pitch dozens and dozens of times.

Canelo Álvarez, though, fought two fights.

How is that possible? Is it because boxing is so popular? Ask yourself: Do you ever hear people talking about boxing? Do you know a bunch of boxing fans? Boxing's TV ratings aren't even in the top-10 most popular sports in the country. The sport ranks way below soccer, for goodness' sake.

Álvarez can make money like that because of one thing: pay-per-view events.

Pay-per-view events are major events that people can buy on a one-off basis and watch at home. And many, many people do!

A few years ago, boxer Floyd Mayweather Jr. made $275 million dollars for a single fight. That's because almost 4.3 million people paid about $100 each to watch the event live.[13]

Don King is a famous boxing promoter, known for his crazy hair and provocative statements. After one fighter got a nine-digit

---

13 Kurt Badenhausen, "How Floyd Mayweather Made a Record $275 Million for One Night of Work," *Forbes*, June 5, 2018, https://www.forbes.com/sites/kurtbadenhausen/2018/06/05/how-floyd-mayweather-earned-275-million-for-one-night-of-work/?sh=72dfcb656e4d.

payout for a single fight, King could hardly believe it. "I mean… that's an entire season of revenue for some [professional] teams!" he stammered.

That's right, Don!

Why does this matter to you? Because now, this same power is in your hands. Maybe the term "online event" or "virtual event" brings up the wrong image. Maybe what comes to mind are half-baked Zoom events, like the ones that popped up right after the shutdown in early 2020. Forget those. They're history. They have nothing to do with what we're talking about now.

Instead, think of it this way. Online event technology is *democratizing pay-per-view* and opening up the same big opportunities. Now, you don't need a dozen satellite trucks. You don't need a deal with Showtime. You don't need to book 500 rooms at the MGM Grand Las Vegas for the support team.

You just need to be able to create a great show that's good enough for people to want to pay for and watch it.

I've seen artists and organizations make a season's or a tour's worth of revenue in one night with an online event.

Again, you might push back and say, "I'm not Canelo Álvarez." And that's true.

But, again, I would bet you don't need to make nearly as much as Canelo brings in from his events to shift the trajectory of your organization. You might not be Floyd "Money" Mayweather, but you could bring in a *lot* less than his $275 million payday and still be pretty happy with it.

Everybody in the live entertainment business can get results with online events. Results that actually matter.

So if it helps, forget the terms "online event" and "virtual event." Think of all this new technology as pay-per-view for everyone. Anyone who can produce a professional show can do a pay-per-view event now.

Over the next few chapters, we're going to sweep away the clouds of mystery so you can see your own path to success. We're moving from *why* to *how*. We'll talk about technical stuff a little bit and cover marketing. The main goal, though, is to show you the major steps you need to take. Imagine that we're standing at home plate, and you've got a bat in your hand. I'm not going to be giving you microscopic pointers on how to stand or the fine points of your swing. I'm going to focus on explaining the rules, telling you what to do after you hit the ball, and pointing out the home-run fence. I'm explaining the game so you can win. You'll fine-tune your swing as you go.

Any professional in this business can succeed with online events. I believe that with no reservations. Soon, very small organizations and individual artists will do shows with seven-digit grosses. Bigger organizations will too, of course.

Anybody, including you, can succeed if you know how to put on a great show.

You've got the bat in your hand. I'm just here to help you knock the ball out of the park.

CHAPTER 4

RESPECT THE MEDIUM

What do you think of when you hear the phrase "online event"?

Within days of the shutdown, live-event creators started putting things online. We all needed some cheering up, some assurance that the world wasn't coming to an end. For most people, these were the first "online events" they had seen. It was fun, in March or April of 2020, to see Bruce Springsteen play songs from his sofa. We were like kids with a new toy, if that kid were trapped in a room and couldn't play with any of the rest of his toys.

Those first events may still be what you think of when you hear "online events." You may even think of "Zoom events" because that's where so many of the early events happened. I'm not knocking Zoom. My hat's off to them. As a communication system, Zoom and others like it were a godsend and stroke of luck for the world. If the pandemic had happened five years earlier, it would have been much harder to muddle through.

But Zoom as a tool for doing a show? Not great. Not even good. It's hard to fault Zoom for this since that was never the goal in the first place. We don't blame hammers for being terrible at putting in screws. And you couldn't really blame someone for using a hammer to put in a screw in an emergency if that's all the person had. And right after the shutdown, it was definitely an emergency.

But suppose someone kept using a hammer long after they'd had time to get a screwdriver. Or they just let all those screws go unscrewed. Then you'd have questions, such as, "Why don't you get a screwdriver?" or "Why do you keep smashing all those screws?" or "Are you just going to sit there and do nothing when you've got all these screws that need to be put in?"

Metaphorically, that's what happened and still happens with online events. Zoom is the wrong tool for an important job when the right tools are available.

So why do people use it for online shows sometimes? Lack of knowledge, for one. That's what this book is trying to help remedy.

But that's not the only reason. People who use Zoom also tend to create mediocre shows. These shows have low production value and little stagecraft. The audience experience is barely thought through. What does the choice of the wrong tool have in common with a less-than-great production?

A lack of respect for the medium.

Why would someone lack respect for the medium?

It could be they fear online events could somehow replace in-person events. (They won't.) It could come from a sense that they or their org are too established to adapt. (They're not.) It could be the belief that delivering good online events needs major technical skills or big money. (It doesn't.) Or it could just come from a sense of overwhelm from trying to survive the pandemic and putting your organization back on track. I understand, believe me.

Finally, some people just don't like online events. And that can create a vicious cycle. People who don't like online events sometimes still have to produce *something* online. Those somethings are usually mediocre at best. Other people watch them, don't enjoy them, and draw the conclusion that online events aren't very good. As a result, when it's their turn to put out an online event, they don't put in the effort. Because online events, as they've learned, are not very good.

The cycle of disrespect is created.

I learned about this cycle from conversations I've had, many of them in the summer or fall of 2020. They often went like this:

ME: What's your thinking about online events at your organization?

LIVE-ENTERTAINMENT EXECUTIVE/TOP MANAGER: We've been doing [table readings/at-home musical performances/rehashes of old content we had lying around] on Zoom.

ME: How are those going?

EXECUTIVE: They're okay. They're never going to replace the in-person experience.

ME: Of course not, but how are they going?

EXECUTIVE: It's hard to say. I think they're good for engagement.[14]

ME: Have you tried selling any?

EXECUTIVE: We did a pay-what-you-can one time.

----

14 When you hear someone say their online events are only to increase "engagement," you can be pretty sure they don't respect the medium.

ME: How'd that go?

EXECUTIVE: Most people didn't pay anything.

ME: What was the event?

EXECUTIVE: It was a short reading of a new play with three actors on Zoom.

ME: [Silent because I'm not able to pretend that sounds interesting.]

EXECUTIVE: So yeah, based on our experience, we don't think people will pay money for these online shows.

ME: What was the production budget on the show you tried to charge for?

EXECUTIVE: Production budget? Well, our Zoom subscription costs $49.95 a month, so we pay for that...

ME: But what about the actual show you were trying to charge money for?

EXECUTIVE: Not much.

ME: If you put more money into the show, you might have more success charging people.

EXECUTIVE: We don't want to do that because nobody pays for online events.

ME: You're saying that based on what happened with your one zero-budget online event?

EXECUTIVE: Yes, we tested online events and learned that nobody will pay for them.[15] So we don't feel comfortable spending money to produce more of them.

ME: Was it a good zero-budget event?

EXECUTIVE: It was okay. These events aren't as good as in-person events, and they never will be.

ME: But you spent basically nothing to make the event, right?

EXECUTIVE: Right.

ME: When you do in-person events, do you spend nothing on those?

EXECUTIVE: Oh, no. They have big budgets. We put everything we can into our shows. We're an artistic organization. That's what it's all about.

ME: And if you skimped on those budgets, what would happen?

EXECUTIVE: People wouldn't buy tickets.

----

15 This is like taking a single match and a cold log and "testing" to see if you can build a fire.

Me: So if you put money into online events…

Executive: People don't pay money for online events.

Me: Based on your experience with your zero-budget event "test."

Executive: Correct. My logic is flawless.

Me: Indeed. [Checks sales report with a long list of online events people are paying for.]

Here's the point: disrespecting the medium means not actually trying to succeed. No one is trying to fail, exactly. They've just set a low bar. They want to say they've done online events. They don't want to be left behind, after all, but they don't really want to keep up either. The result is that the work they produce isn't all that great, and because of that, people don't show up or don't want to pay much for it. Creators who do this get the cause and effect backwards.

They think the *cause* is that online events aren't worth their time, and so the *effect* is that they don't put in the effort.

In fact, their belief that online events aren't worth their time is the *cause*. The *effect* is that their events are not very good.

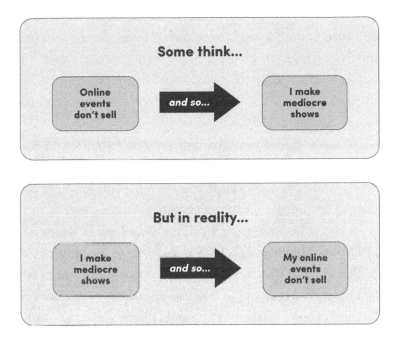

THE ONE LAW OF RESPECTING THE ONLINE MEDIUM

I get it. I spent the first month or two of the pandemic observing all the bad events. After the novelty of sofa-based concerts wore off, I thought to myself, *These events suck, and as soon as we don't have to, we won't do these anymore.* I was not bullish.

Then, in April of 2020, I saw a few creators who took the medium more seriously, and the difference was night and day. Hershey Felder, for example, did a truly live concert from a beautiful theatre in Italy. It had a multi-camera set up with excellent-quality video, some nicely worked in video effects, and great sound. It was a compelling, well-thought-through hour and a half of music and fun with the audience. In other words, a live show that anyone in the world could watch.

He audaciously charged real money for it ($50 or so, if I recall), and I actually advised his team to lower that price. They rejected my advice, and it's a good thing they did because the show sold. And sold. And sold! Hershey did great business on that show. People loved it, and he continued to deliver more shows. He's got fans and supporters who continue to show up, enjoy what he does, and pay for the privilege.

He wasn't the only one, though. Josh Groban, Richard Marx, and other musicians safely delivered excellent, fully realized, live shows. And fans showed up! It was eye-opening to me, and I changed my tune on the future potential of online events.

In fact, it inspired what I call the **One Law of Respecting the Online Medium**: *make a great show and charge people to see it.*

That's it. And what you'll notice about this law is that it's what you *always* do. You're in the business of making great shows and charging people for them. It shouldn't be any different online. The ways you make and sell the show change a little, but the very simple principle behind them is exactly the same. For some reason, live-event creators forgot this after the shutdown. Those days made lasting impressions on us all. But by now, more and more producers have returned to their senses. When it comes to online events, make a show worth paying for, and people will pay.

THOSE WHO DON'T KNOW HISTORY...

I've seen this before, by the way, this lack of respect for a new medium. I've been working in the internet business since the late '90s. At that time, many companies showed their lack of respect for the internet by ignoring it. Or they stuck a toe in the water. They built toothless, bland "brochure" websites. They didn't do e-commerce, even though they sold things for a living. These companies always blamed their customers, of course. They claimed their audience didn't use the web because:

a. They were too old and didn't understand the technology.

b. They wanted to talk to a person when they bought something.

c. They didn't trust putting their credit card into a computer.

d. All of the above.

It was a wall of disrespect that stopped them from doing anything. A few years later, of course, they pretty much had to establish a presence online. By this time, they'd been lapped by competitors and spent a decade or more playing catch up, if they ever did catch up. Some never did. Remember Toys R Us?[16] Neither do I.

It happened again 10 years later or so with the mobile revolution. Business owners would claim no one was buying on their mobile devices and never would. If they built a mobile website at all, they made sure it was almost completely useless and haphazardly designed.

I fell into this same trap when I decided we should build a limited version of Goldstar for our first app. We called it "Goldstar Weekend." We meant for it to be a companion to the website with less functionality. Robin to the website's Batman. But we weren't even halfway through building Goldstar Weekend when I realized our mistake. Face in palm. We didn't need a "companion" app. We needed a world-beating, event-selling machine. Not long after, we

---

16 Denise Dahlhoff and Mark A. Cohen, "What Went Wrong: The Demise of Toys R Us," Knowledge@Wharton blog, University of Pennsylvania Wharton School of Business, March 14, 2018, https://knowledge.wharton.upenn.edu/article/the-demise-of-toys-r-us/.

threw away Goldstar Weekend and launched the Goldstar app as soon as we could. Only a couple years later, most of our sales and traffic came from our mobile web users and the app. The company was set up for success in a new generation.

Others chose a different path, but none of the mobile-web refusers are still around. I could tell you about two or three competitors that went out of business despite being well-funded. And the day that they did, they still had no app in the app store.

No respect for the new medium.

FEAR IS A BAD TEACHER

We can check the historical record to see other common ways people respond to change in their industry.

At first, most people try to copy and paste the old medium into the new medium, and we'll talk more about that later.

The second thing people do is worry. Many assume the new medium will damage the old medium. It's an understandable reaction. Something younger and sexier has come along, and it's going to ruin a perfectly good relationship.

But this fear is unhelpful for two reasons. First, the emergence of a new medium rarely lays waste to the old media in the way the old media imagine it might.

In the early 20th century, for example, the denizens of the sheet music industry were freaked out. Records were going to be the death of them. Why would people buy sheet music and play it at home if they could listen to a record? Anyone could go to a phonograph parlor and take a listen for just pennies.

But the sheet music industry is worth $1 billion in the US alone per year. I came across articles describing it as a "booming industry."[17] So what gives? Weren't they supposed to be dead 100 years ago?

This cycle repeated itself throughout the 20th and 21st centuries. Radio was supposed to kill records. TV was supposed to kill radio. Cable was supposed to kill broadcast. The internet was supposed to kill everything, and the mobile internet would wipe out anything still left alive after that.

But what do you notice about the story that I just told? Every medium I just described still has tens of millions of users or more in the US alone. True, they've changed forms, and some have waned. But if sheet music, for example, is still "booming" after 120 years of being in the line of fire from new technologies, what does that tell us? It tells us that maybe that fear instinct when faced with a new medium needs a little tuning.

The second reason fear is unhelpful is because it keeps us from learning from what's changing and adjusting course appropriately.

All we have to do is look at the story of recorded music to understand why this matters so much. Records, then eight-tracks, then cassettes, then CDs dominated the last three or four decades of the 20th century. If you were a success in the "music" business, you were going to be famous, make a fortune, or both. And then an innovation came along that brought it all down at high speed. Napster and file-sharing hit the recorded music industry like a quick-acting poison. Recorded music (mostly CDs, but also cassettes and LPs) brought in revenue of over $14 billion in 1999.[18]

- - - - - - - - - - - -

17 Matt Hunckler, "MusicSpoke Looks to Disrupt $1 Billion Sheet Music Industry with Marketplace for Artist-Owned Scores," *Forbes*, October 25, 2017, https://www.forbes.com/sites/matthunckler/2017/10/25/musicspoke-looks-to-disrupt-1-billion-sheet-music-industry-with-marketplace-for-artist-owned-scores/?sh=4927790d5eb2.

18 All music industry size data comes from the RIAA's database, which is currently found at https://www.riaa.com/u-s-sales-database/.

A decade later, in 2010, that number was cut in half. CD sales, the gold mine of the recorded-music biz, had gone from $12.8 billion to just $3.4 billion during that time.

Let's dwell on that for a second. The music industry's reaction to Napster was pretty much all-out panic. Feeling the fear of elimination, they protected the golden goose at all costs. They even sued individual customers for downloading files from places like Napster. Their approach—denial, self-righteousness, and enforcement—sent people into the arms of evermore unbeatable file-sharing services. This drove industry revenue down, down, down. The industry bigwigs were standing athwart the flow of history yelling, "Stop!" but history ignored them and kept flowing, just like it always does.

They could have known they were picking the wrong approach. History is full of clear examples. But when you're that successful, it doesn't feel like history applies to you.

Eventually, of course, on the verge of being wiped out, they changed their tune. They embraced digital downloads and then streaming subscription services. This all could have happened back in 2000, but it didn't. As a result, recorded music industry total sales didn't reach their 1999 level again until...well, actually, they still haven't as of 2021. But they've risen! Mostly because of streaming-subscription revenue (Spotify, etc.), the music industry is all the way back to 1994. And industry revenue was "only" 25 percent down in 2019 from the peak a generation ago. Let's ignore inflation so we don't feel too sorry for them, shall we?[19]

---

19 If you did consider inflation, recorded music industry revenue was actually down 50 percent in 2019 versus 1999, even with the massive growth in subscription-services money. On an inflation-adjusted basis, revenue dropped as low as 32 percent of 1999 in 2015, before the subscription-service revenues really kicked in.

I took this detour because we're facing a similar moment in the live business. History's most important lesson for this moment is this: the biggest threat to an existing industry when faced with a new medium is how the leaders of that industry react to it.

But I'm here to tell you something that might surprise you. I've spent the last couple years talking to the masters of the "old" medium of in-person events. They are *not* behaving the way the music industry leaders did back in 2000. It's a mixed bag, but minds are open, not closed. We have the pandemic to thank for that, but that doesn't matter. Change happens how it happens, usually in response to pressure. And few industries have ever faced as much pressure as the live business faced from Covid.

Generally, leaders in the industry have embraced online events in concept. They see both the possibilities and the threats and are wisely choosing to invest. If that continues, online events will keep growing and contribute to the success of the live business.

If it changes, if leaders stop investing, that's when the danger starts.

THE FRIENDLY, REASONABLE REVOLUTIONARIES

It's not just people currently in the business who are paying attention. Young creatives, in particular, see the emergence of a new medium for what it is: an opportunity to rise. They know it isn't easy to get a break in the music business or on Broadway, whether as an artist or on the business side. They know those in the halls of power aren't super eager to give up their power or share it with an upstart. That message has been received quite clearly. When it comes to live events, the chaos of a new medium crashing into an old medium creates the opportunity some are looking for. "Chaos," to quote *Game of Thrones*, "is a ladder."

Mind you, the creative crowd I'm talking about doesn't mean any harm to anyone. They don't really want the VP of Marketing at Such-and-Such Performing Arts Center's job. They just want to do interesting and creative work in the field they love. They want to build their reputations and make a good income, possibly without being beholden to the existing power structure. This may be especially true for women, people of color, and others who can hardly find a crack in the facade of the status quo in which to create the tiniest bit of space for themselves.

It's not that they don't have the chops. It's that structurally, it might take 20 years for them just to get a look in, as the British say. A chance would be a fine thing.

So, yes, if you're an incumbent, there is a threat, but it's not from barbarians at the gate. I've met the people in that creative group looking to shake up the industry, and they're not barbarians. They're great people with a lot to add to the industry. If you're an incumbent, you should be building relationships with them because they see where this is going. They understand the power this new medium can give them, and if you won't work with them or give them opportunities, eventually they'll create opportunities for themselves.

The only real threat is within. The phone call is coming from inside the house. Answer it because it's future-you on the other end of the line saying, "Take online events seriously!"

In other words, *make great online shows and charge people to see them.*

Of course, it's not quite that simple. Almost, but there are a few new things you'll need to actively do now that you've taken the first step of respecting the medium.

CHAPTER 5

LEARN THE TECH

Sometimes, the word "technology" intimidates people.

It sounds like something special, something from an alien planet. Or it has the connotation of something magical, inscrutable. For nerds or the very young, it may be second nature. But it's a showstopper for others. It's an ugly barrier to doing the "real work," whatever that may be.

Except all of that is nonsense. Nonsense and malarky and other less-polite words too. The mystique of technology serves some people's purposes just fine. It keeps the "unenlightened" relying on the services of the select few who get it.

But technology is just a fancy-sounding word for knowing how to do something. A stick is hot-dog-cooking technology. Putting your right foot in, putting your right foot out, putting your right foot in, and shaking it all about is doing-the-hokey-pokey technology. And when it comes to online events, there are a few new things you do need to know how to do that you might not know right now.

I've been in the "technology" business since the Clinton administration. I've led teams and companies that built and operated internet-based things. I'm not a "technical" person, but I'm not ignorant either. I couldn't code my way out of a paper bag, but I also know enough to call shenanigans when necessary.

That's what I want for you when it comes to online events. That's the purpose of this chapter. It's not to make you a propeller head.

So if you already know the ins and outs of filming and streaming or if you're already a pro, skip this chapter. It's going to be redundant for you. And I'm probably going to say something wrong or oversimplified and annoy you. Fair enough. I stand corrected. You can jump straight to the chapter on marketing.

I'd like to thank the two professionals on my own team who helped me structure this chapter. Between the two of them, they've helped people stream thousands of shows.

If you're still here, that means you're not a pro and you want to learn more. Awesome! Let's go!

WHAT TO THINK ABOUT FIRST

The first thing to consider is the content you, or your organization, are streaming. This drives everything, really. A one-woman show on a small stage needs one set of things. A major outdoor concert with several stages needs another. In a way, the first question is an artistic one. What would create the best experience of this event for the audience?

Taking our examples, a one-woman show on a small stage needs proper lighting and clear sound. We need to see the performer and the sets, and we probably don't want just one angle on the show the whole time. We want to zoom in on her face sometimes to capture an expression or punctuate a joke. We want to pan as she moves across the stage too. We might even have some simple dramatic lighting effects to show mood. We can use light and sound to dramatize something that happens. We could do more, but that's not a bad start.

A big outdoor concert with several stages needs quite a bit more. Lots of cameras, including some flying over the audience. Elaborate miking and mixing of the musicians. Probably a host stand with a whole set up for the host, including guest interviewees. Graphics packages between performers. Pyrotechnics, if it's a certain kind of show. You get the idea. The needs are much more extensive.

In each example, the show content drives the requirements for streaming. When you think of it that way, it's easier to wrap your head around. The questions begin to answer themselves.

Remember too that streaming literally happens all the time from just about everywhere. People are streaming content in every conceivable form every second of every day. Concerts by the dozens happen daily. People on rollerblades stream their thoughts as they cruise past the beach. People stream themselves talking while they play video games. And tens of thousands of fans are watching. People stream things like the bird feeder in their front yard. (That's me.)

To paraphrase Snoop Dogg, streaming ain't nothing but a thing. As a matter of fact, it's such a common thing you can learn to do it without too much effort.

WHAT IS A VIDEO STREAM, ACTUALLY?

Streaming and filming are a lot alike. Chances are, if it works on film, it works on a stream. If the cameras and mics are a good fit for recording something, they are a good fit for streaming it.

Note that "archival filming" is not what I am talking about. People do archival filming to keep a record of a live show. This is in case the aliens attack, and we need a record of human civilization (I guess).

I'm talking about filming the way you'd want to see something as a viewer. If you can do that, you can stream.

If you're streaming, the sound and video hit the mic and camera, and the information gets digitized. That means it gets transformed, via complicated math, into a bunch of signals that go into your hardware and software set up.

Your setup then takes that digital signal and encodes it into a stream. That signal goes to the cloud, which sounds fluffy and soft but is just a server on the internet.

That server does more math and turns your encoded signal into an even more specially encoded signal. But not just because it can. The cloud-based server *reencodes (technically transcodes) your audio and video content into the appropriate formats* for your viewers. It makes your stream work on all the phones, computers, tablets, and smart TVs they own.

Wherever they are, your viewers connect to the internet. As they do, they're *downloading lots of tiny, little video files.* The device they're using then *puts all those files back together* so they run smoothly and in order.

It's pretty amazing that it works when you think about it, but it does!

As I said, people stream stuff all the time. The number of videos that people stream successfully and beautifully blows my mind. Netflix alone streams an estimated 23,269 *years'* worth of content to its customers in a single day.[20] Talk about binge-watching!

Once the signal leaves your building, so to speak, you shouldn't have to worry about it anymore. Streaming technology is mature and stable if you're on a professional platform. Though deliverability problems do exist, the fact is we all rely on streaming all day

---

20 "Netflix Subscribers Likely Streaming More than 200 Million Hours Daily," Finley, accessed August 10, 2021, https://finleyusa.com/netflix-subscribers-likely-streaming-more-than-200-million-hours-daily/.

long. A streaming platform like Stellar runs on the same reliable, mega-scale networks (like Amazon AWS or Microsoft's Azure) as Netflix and Disney do.

Choose your platform carefully! No "home brew" video delivery system should be considered. This is not the place to be cheap or "creative."

WHAT YOU DO NEED TO WORRY ABOUT

Beside picking the right platform, there are a few other things you have to do right. As mentioned, the artistic requirements drive many of the technical requirements. As a nontechnical person who has worked with artists and technical people for a long time, I believe in creative briefs. If you're responsible for developing a show, including making sure the technical requirements are right, you'll need a team that has those technical skills, and a good creative brief is the best way to get the best work out of them.

In the brief, you include the core requirements, of course. But you have to go further and include the impression you're trying to create, the vibe. It's wise to follow this with a long, rambling description of what you're after. When in doubt, include it. A document like this helps set the table for success.

After that, have a nice long talk with the technical team. Talk it out. If you've got a good team, they should be able to figure out what you'll need technically to execute on the vision. Don't skip this step.

If you don't have the option of getting the help of a technical team, you'll have to educate yourself more on these issues. Even if you do it yourself, starting with a creative brief still makes sense. It's a way to clarify what you're trying to do, even to yourself.

The real goal is to make the viewers forget the technology. That's your concern. They should never give a moment's thought about the gear you're using or the platform it's on. You want it to be pure bliss. Like butter. As frictionless as listening to a radio. Easy like Sunday morning.

If your audio/video set up is good and your platform is good, you need one more thing: **good internet**. I said before that once the signal leaves your building, your worries are over. That's true. But you do have to make sure your *content leaves your building fast enough*. Here's what you need for that:

- A computer with *enough processing power* to encode the stream.

- A *hard–wired (not Wi–Fi) connection to the internet.*[21]

- An upload speed of *at least 10 mbps (megabits per second).*[22]

Not having any one of these is a major streaming pitfall. Without them, the signal will have a hard time getting out of the building and into that magic, math-doing cloud.

Don't be a statistic on this one. If you're using Stellar, we're always happy to help you do a tech check if you've got an upcoming Stellar show. But no matter the platform you're using, don't do a show without *knowing with certainty that these things will not be a problem*. This is a literal potential showstopper, a show-bufferer, whatever you want to call it. It's a gut-wrenching and

- - - - - - - - - - -

21 I'm writing this in the year 2021. 5G may change this in the not-too-distant future, but still… make sure.

22 Specifically, this is for 1080p video. You may actually need more. Again, I hope that you're reading this in the future laughing. "My toaster's upload speed is faster than that!" Still…make sure.

easily avoidable nightmare. Like scurvy. Eat your lemons, and skip the whole problem.

If you've covered all of that, you can spend most of your effort on the content and the experience. It's time to share your awesomeness with the world!

IS THIS GOING TO BE EXPENSIVE?

Spending some money on production does make a difference, but you don't need a huge budget. You are shooting for what's called "broadcast-quality audio and video." It's a little bit of an outdated term, I realize. It makes me think about old-fashioned TV stations and satellite dishes. That may help, though. Picture a news broadcast at a local TV station. You can deliver what they're delivering (better, actually) with a lot less cost, effort, and money. And more creativity. And a lot less hair spray, probably.

What I'm about to describe is true for any production. Whether you've got a massive performing arts center and its staff at your disposal or you're a scrappy entrepreneur, the basic structure for broadcast quality audio and video is the same.

Here are the basic requirements:[23]

- Cameras

- Lights

- Microphones

---

23 Again, this list may look ridiculous if you're reading this too far into the future. Can you believe we used to have cameras that didn't levitate on their own?

- A way to mix them together. Software like OBS is excellent and free, but there are other choices.

- A way to encode all this content and send it up to the cloud.

You can do this at literally any budget. You could do a decent online event with things you probably already have. You could also spend a million dollars on this equipment. If you'd like some input, contact us at Stellar, and we can talk you through what you need and what you can do with what you have.

I won't kid you, though. Shooting a show on an iPhone is possible, but unless it's highly artistic, it will likely fall short of your viewers' expectations. Having said that, a little bit of money (even just a couple thousand dollars) goes a long, long way. And frankly, you don't even have to buy this gear. Almost anywhere in the world, you can rent all this equipment at a reasonable price.

You can also avoid spending money on things that don't add value. Shooting in 4K, for example, drives costs up considerably, but almost nobody can see it. Few people have devices or internet connections that can even handle 4K. However, 4K video *will* increase the cost and difficulty of your video capture. So it's worth considering whether something like 4K video is a good decision.

Everything comes back to the viewer's experience. That's how you should determine where you'll invest money, not waste it. Bad lighting, a static camera, no-good mics, and janky internet may save you a little money. But I guarantee your viewers will notice.

You don't have to be Stanley Kubrick, but you do have to put on a good show.

IF YOU "KNOW NOTHING ABOUT COMPUTERS"

If this information is blowing your mind or making you want to stress eat a box of doughnuts, don't panic.

I want to reassure you of one very important thing: **you don't have to learn a bunch of complicated technology to be successful with online events.**

Your role will determine how likely you are to be hands-on with the technology for online events. Unless you're wearing all the hats or your one hat is the technical hat, you can probably avoid having to learn the details.

If you want to learn the tech in depth, you can. It's a great opportunity for some people to build their professional skills right now. But you don't have to if that's not you or it doesn't make sense in your role.

Put that Dunkin' box down.

If you are a person who "knows nothing about computers" but still wants to be an online event success story, you've got two choices.

First, you can easily learn what you need to know, and you don't have to go any further than YouTube. You can search for anything and everything related to streaming and what you'd need to be able to do to successfully produce an online event. Do you want to know how to configure a camera? There's a YouTube video for that. Do you want to know how to do green screens like a pro? YouTube!

Second, do you want to *not* do any of that? You don't have to. Even if you're budget constrained, there are people you can hire to do this stuff for you. If you're less budget constrained, I *recommend* you hire people to do this stuff for you. They have experience and expertise that will improve your shows considerably.

Either way, take a deep breath, and say it with me: You. Can. Do. This.

The "technology" of online events shouldn't be a barrier. It shouldn't even, after a little while, be much of a consideration. It's just the toolset for the important thing. The show. The one that the whole world is waiting to see.

We'll talk about that show and how to market it in the next chapter.

CHAPTER 6

MARKETING YOUR ONLINE EVENT

"This changes everything."

People use that phrase a lot these days. Steve Jobs loved it. He used it so much it became the tagline of the Apple iPhone 4 launch.

People have said other things have "changed everything" too. I did a quick search and found an allergy spray and a coffee creamer that said their new products changed everything. A church said their new music service did. Others said climate change and the pandemic did.

Some of the things on that list do seem pretty big, at least compared to coffee creamer. But with all these examples, one thing is true.

Even the pandemic and other mega-forces didn't change *everything.*

I think it's important to start here when thinking about marketing. We'll look at ways marketing has changed, but let's start with how it's the same it's always been. The basic laws of physics still apply.

THE MOST IMPORTANT THING

Let's start with the most basic of those basic laws: you have to design your marketing plan to do what you need it to do.

That may sound stupid, but it's not. Many marketing plans for live shows are not designed to work unless a miracle occurs. Why? Because what's in the plan cannot achieve the sales results needed for the show to be a success. Without a miracle.

I call this a "six-foot ladder." I coined this term years ago in frustration when someone brought me a plan that had no chance of working. I said, "It's like I asked you for a way to get over a 10-foot wall, and you brought me a six-foot ladder."

A six-foot ladder looks like something you'd use to climb a 10-foot wall. But it's not actually designed for the task. It won't work because it can't work. Unless a giant eagle carries you over the wall once you're at the top of the ladder.

A 10-foot wall needs at least a 10-foot ladder. Marketers create six-foot ladders because they don't know how to build 10-foot ladders. But they can do six-footers all day long.

You may have less certainty that your 10-foot ladder will work. It's going to be harder to build. But if you build it, you can climb the wall. Now you have a solution that actually can work. Without needing a miracle.

THE TOOLS YOU'LL USE, IN ORDER OF PREFERENCE

You've got limitless ways to reach customers, in theory. In practice, you'll probably use these three tools the most. They're in order of preference. What I mean by that is you should start with the top and work your way down. Most of the time, you'll need all three.

Tap into Your Existing Audience First

Every super-successful online event I've ever seen taps an existing audience. If you have loyal supporters or customers you can reach, start with those. If the artist or show or venue has an audience, they're going to be the cornerstone of your plan.

If you've got a big enough audience, your job is easy. Start with your own email lists and social media followers. This is your best audience by far.

Still, you have to build a plan to reach them. Be creative. Map it out on the calendar. One touch point is never enough to get the full value from an audience, and you have to speak to them in their language. They're fans and followers, so spend time crafting messages that connect with them. More than any other potential prospects, they're on your side already.

What if you don't have an existing audience? It's going to be harder the first time out, but that's okay. You can use your first event to *build* an audience for future events. You can do a series or similar production later, so don't miss the opportunity. Later, you'll be able to leverage and serve the audience you're working hard to build now.

If you do, it's like compounding interest. Every show will start on a higher footing than the last. Do this long enough, and these events will become insanely popular and profitable. You know...if you're into that kind of thing.

Partners, Friends, and Allies

After you've put your existing audience to full use, the next best tool is to put *other people's* audiences to use.

They promote your show to the people who pay attention to them. Sometimes they'll do this for you for free just because they like what you do. More often, you'll need to pay them. In my view, the investment is usually worth it. You get to help other people prosper for helping you!

It's easy to set this up. Stellar and other systems generate a unique trackable link that you give to a partner. They send traffic through that link and earn a pre-agreed share of the revenue they create. A literal win-win.

Not everyone will do this for you. You'll need to pay some of them a fixed amount. This works more like buying an ad, but if you pick your partners right, it's still beneficial. They have the special attention of the people they reach. If those people are likely to care about what *you* do too, you'll probably get a nice return on your investment.

In this step, you'll be dealing with organizations and companies as well as individuals. These could be personalities or influencers. You should look for the ones who *believe in and like* what you're doing. That makes it more likely they will want to support you and less likely they're just in it for the dough.

Though again, if they're making some nice money, that doesn't hurt your cause. They will feel even better about supporting you.

Doing this takes hustle and research, and that's why fewer people do it than you'd imagine. It's easier just to buy ads. But that extra effort is worth it because the people that you tend to reach this way are "warmer." Their connection to whoever's sending the message is stronger than it would be to any old ad.

On average, in fact, a marketing dollar spent this way is about *twice* as effective as a dollar spent on paid ads, based on the data I've seen since we started Stellar.

Twice as effective!

You're also putting money in the pockets of people you like more than Google and Facebook. They've got plenty already.

Paid Online Ads, Probably on Google and Facebook

Most online events also need to do some paid advertising, and it's not a bad idea. There are some advantages that go along with the expense and risk.

You want to run "online ads" and not just "ads" because you're selling an online product. That's where you should focus your paid advertising.

To be more specific though, it's search and social. To be even more specific than that, it's pretty much just Google and Facebook. (Remember that YouTube is also Google and Instagram is also Facebook.)

Yes, we live in a dystopian advertising duopoly, but that's where we are. On the plus side, these two companies have built some effective ways for you to reach people.

I'd be foolish to lay out a step-by-step Google and Facebook strategy here. That kind of info is everywhere, but let's connect it to your goals.

First, you can use the existing audience and data you've got to get more out of your paid ads. The advertising tools change all the time, but at least a couple of features should be available to you.

Look-alike audiences. If you've got an existing audience and the data to go with it, you can find more people like them. Definitely use that feature.

Targeting and interest data. This is the bread and butter of online ads. It works well in combination with the data you own too. Test, track, and see what gets a response. Be relentless, especially at first, to see what works.

My main point here is that you will need to use all three tools, including paid online ads, for nearly every show. No shame in that game. These are the three main horses you will ride to victory.

Remember, though, that the *tools* of marketing do not constitute a marketing *plan.* You have to think through and map out how you will use them to get the results you want. Your in-person experience helps a lot here, but if you need help, don't worry. Consultants and companies exist that specialize in planning and managing marketing plans.

THREE IMPORTANT DIFFERENCES

Now let's talk about some differences between online and in-person event marketing. They're not particularly hard to grasp, but you should know them.

Give Yourself Enough Time

People buy tickets to online events later than they do for in-person events. That's a fact. The following graph includes data from thousands of shows that have been on Stellar, and you can see the trend.

Online Event Sales By Days Before Event

All Event Types

Based On All Stellar Sales Through March 2021

It makes sense, of course. Good tickets don't sell out for online events, and there's less planning required to "go" to an online event. This has an impact on how people buy.

But I've heard people say some crazy things about how late customers buy their tickets for online events. One guy told me he was expecting 95 percent of his sales to happen on the day of the show.

It didn't, and I've never seen anything close to 95 percent day-of sales. Take stories like that with a grain of salt. It wouldn't shock me to see even 50 percent the same day, which is much higher than the average.

But here's the key thing. Late buying does *not* mean late marketing.

This is a common misconception. I've fallen into the trap of waiting too long to start marketing an online show and learned the hard way how it cuts down your chances of success.

You should plan on six to eight weeks of marketing for your show, and more if possible.

Too many times, I've seen people try to rush. It never works.

Just because people *buy* late doesn't mean you can wait to *reach* them.

Think of it like a garden. You're planting seeds and cultivating the garden. The harvest comes later, and there's nothing you can do to rush it. And if you don't plan, water, or cultivate, you won't grow anything at all.

And the last minute is a terrible time to start a garden. Wasn't there an Aesop's fable about that?

Give yourself enough time for a bountiful harvest.

Local Is Less Important; Enthusiastic Is More Important

I love going to in-person events, and I'll go to just about anything. I don't have to be a mega-fan to go see a show rather than sit at home.

For in-person events, people like me are valuable. Just being "local" makes someone a decent potential buyer.

On the other hand, nonlocals make terrible target customers for in-person events. And virtually the whole world is nonlocals. How can you sell a ticket to someone who's not there to see a show?

For in-person event marketing, "local" is essential.

For online events, local means little. Anyone in the world is a potential buyer.

But how do you market to "anyone"?

You don't. With online events, place is less important, but enthusiasm for the show is more important. The online event marketer doesn't have to worry about where someone is. The job is to reach the enthusiastic person *wherever they are.*

Some people will go to a concert, for example, because the weather's nice. Or because the venue has a nice bar. Or the band has one or two songs they know.

With online events, you're looking for a customer that's more enthusiastic about the content itself. A good cocktail and a summer night don't sell tickets to online shows. That's how you draw casual fans to in-person events, but it doesn't work for online events.

Enthusiasm for the artist or show does work for online events. Anywhere in the world, a fan is a good target.

So as you make your marketing plans, remember this inversion. The way to think about your target customer gets flipped upside down.

Plan accordingly.

Don't Expect Financial Miracles

Here's a rule of thumb about online-event marketing: on average, every dollar spent on marketing translates to $2 to $3 in revenue.

I gathered data from Stellar on as many shows as I could to learn this. I took the actual revenue for a show and then divided it by the total marketing costs. I averaged that number for a bunch of shows.

If a show sold $10,000 in revenue on a marketing budget of $3,500, each marketing dollar produced $2.85 in revenue. That's just an example, but it's in the average range based on what I've seen.

Shows go way above and below that $2 to $3 range, but you can't assume yours will. If your plan assumes your marketing productivity will be well above this range, it could be a problem. You could be building one of those six-foot ladders.

I saw a marketing budget that assumed each dollar would produce $11 in revenue! Is it possible? Sure, but not very likely. The show's budget was unrealistic unless a miracle occurred.

I'm sharing this info so you can set yourself up for success and not disappointment.

Not every show will fall into the average range. Some people are great marketers or start with very strong existing audiences. Other shows don't have an existing audience, which makes it harder. Or bad luck means early marketing just doesn't land with consumers.

But you should be aware of what you need and what your plan is relying on.

To avoid a nasty surprise, find your own number for a planned show. What revenue are you targeting? Divide that by the marketing budget you've got in mind. Check your number below to see where that puts you:

RATIO	WHAT THIS MEANS
<$2	You might be spending too much on marketing. Or you may be in the right range if you're starting with no existing audience.
$2–$3	This is average. Watch your actual results as you go to adjust up or down. You're probably in the right ballpark though.
$3–$5	This might work if you've got a strong existing audience. Lots of good revenue-sharing arrangements with partners can get you here too. Or this can work if you're just a really, really good marketer. Don't get cocky.
$5<	You're relying on miracles. Or you are three-time Tony- and Grammy-winner Lin-Manuel Miranda.

This table isn't gospel. It's feedback on your plan. Your results will be your own, and you should try to outperform the averages. Don't let this data get in the way of your greatness. Do your thing.

It's true you don't have to spend big money to be effective. It's true money is no guarantee of marketing success.

But it's also true the right amount of well-spent marketing money correlates strongly to revenue.

For online events, this is what I've learned about how to budget and plan for success.

As you go, you'll add your own marketing innovations to the mix. Experiment. Measure. Tweak. It's early days for this medium, and we've all still got a lot to learn.

We know enough to keep going, though. We know for sure that events with poor or no marketing plans will almost definitely fail.

In the next chapter, we're going to finish this part of the book with a checklist. It's an anti-failure checklist: five things that virtually guarantee your event won't flop. This will help you avoid failure and increase your chances of success.

The one thing all successful events have in common is that they didn't fail.

Ready? Let's go.

CHAPTER 7

HOW TO MAKE SURE YOUR EVENT DOESN'T FAIL

L et's put this together.

It can be overwhelming to think about everything you've got to do to create an online event. Especially when you're new at it, the list of things you've got to get right can seem long.

So rather than having to remember a million things you've got to do right, let's focus on a few things to avoid doing wrong. Avoid failure to achieve success.

And with that, here are my Big 5 for online event success:

1. BASE YOUR EVENT ON AN *ARTIST OR SHOW WITH A BUILT-IN FOLLOWING.*

You don't need a mega-star, but it helps a lot to have a performer or show that's got people who already care about it. This is what we called an "existing audience" in the marketing chapter.

Notice that I said an artist or show with a following. I didn't say an artist or show that's *famous*. Those seem similar, but they're not one and the same. There are big names, well-known names, with very little in the way of an active fan base or people that you can reach. By contrast, some shows and artists aren't super famous, but they have a strong, reachable following. Obviously, very well-known *and* with an active fan base is the best combination, but this may not always be possible.

If you don't have an existing audience, you'll need to go further down the list of marketing tools, but that's okay. It's a colder start and somewhat riskier, but you can still do it. But if you can, build your show around an existing audience!

2. BUILD *HIGH PRODUCTION VALUE PER DOLLAR* INTO THE SHOW.

Quality matters, and that's not just about the budget. The show needs to have impact artistically and be something worth watching, period. There aren't any special rules or exceptions the patron will make just because it's an online event. It still has to be exciting. It still has to be engaging, well-written, and well-performed.

We talked about the early online events that producers more or less threw together. They weren't very good. But you're not going to produce those. If you take online events seriously, you'll build on your usual standard of excellence.

You'll need to wring out any costs that don't contribute to production value. Many producers have created excellent shows on limited budgets. They still appeal to lots of people and have major revenue-generating potential. I'm not saying do it on a shoestring. I'm saying do it well, do it right, but do it smart. Start your planning by thinking about *High Production Value per Dollar.*

3. CREATE A *SOLID MARKETING PLAN.*

The biggest pitfall in marketing online events that I've seen is not marketing at all. The second biggest pitfall is marketing without a strong enough plan.

Go down the list we created in the marketing chapter. Start with your existing audiences, and keep going. Make a plan. Put dates, activities, and dollars on it.

Does your plan have a chance to succeed? Or are you building a six-foot ladder for a 10-foot problem? Make sure you're building a 10-foot ladder, and then get to work.

4. *MAKE SURE YOU'VE GOT THE PROPER TECH SETUP AND DO A FULL PRE-CHECK.*

If you've done the things we've already discussed, you're on track to succeed. Your technology can ruin it. That's why you must make sure your tech is going to work. If you use a service like Stellar, you don't have to worry about having too many people show up and crushing the system. Stellar is built on the same platform as many of the world's largest streaming companies, so no sweat there.

What you need to test and check is how you'll be sending the show's content to Stellar. We covered this in the tech chapter, so review that list.

Don't be shy about getting professional help here. You should feel 100 percent confident in your technology on the day of the show. Hire someone to walk you through it. At Stellar, we provide a Streamcoach to do your tech check with you. But no matter what platform you're using, make double-dog sure you know well in advance that your setup is ready. Nothing brings a party to a halt like technical issues.

I can't emphasize this enough. Don't leave this to chance! Pre-check your tech!

5. PROVIDE A *GREAT SHOW-GOING EXPERIENCE!*

You're almost there. It's showtime! What's left? Just one thing. People come to an online event the same way they come to an in-person event. They're excited! They're looking to have a great time and experience the magic of live entertainment! And they might occasionally have a question or even a problem or two. It happens, right?

What are the keys to making sure your customers have a great experience all around? First, you want your ticketing to be smooth and efficient. People should be able to get into the show easily and quickly while still having ticket security. They should be able to get help if they need it, with "front of house"-style service for their questions.

The stream itself should be reliable but also high quality. The audio-video should come through as well as anything on any streaming service. Not only that, but viewers should be able to watch it where they like. Some will watch on a phone. Most won't. They'll want a more relaxed viewing experience and use either their computer or a smart TV app. Make sure they can.

And finally, make it fun and energetic. Pre-show chat has proven to be one of the most exciting aspects of online events. On Stellar, the stream lobby opens an hour before the show, and it's a fun place to be! Watching the emoji-based reactions fly up the screen—applause, high-fives, hearts, and so forth—brings the whole show to life. People have a blast interacting with each other even before the show starts.

And there's even more you can do. I've seen pre-show trivia, prize giveaways, and more. You can dream up your own stuff. The important thing is that people want to have a good time. Your job is to make that happen.

Okay, so let's review our **Big 5 for online event success**:

1. Base your event on a show or artist with an existing following, if possible.

2. Create high production value per dollar in your budget.

3. Build and execute a solid marketing plan.

4. Get your tech setup right and confirm it with a tech check or technical rehearsal.

5. And finally, give the people a great show-going experience.

If you do all five of these things, your event stands an excellent chance of succeeding and being a big hit.

We've covered *why* you should do online events. We've covered *how* you do them and how you avoid failure. In the next section, we're going to explore *what* you can do.

Online events come in different forms. Your goals and capabilities will determine which ones make sense for you. Let's take a look!

PART 3

WHAT

PREAMBLE: CRISIS AT THE WORLD'S FAIR

It was 1904, and Arnold was an ice cream maker working the St. Louis World's Fair. Ice cream was very popular in America, and there were 50 other ice cream vendors at the fair besides Arnold. Even with all this supply, though, trade was brisk. Over 20 million people would come to the fair from all over the world. That made it a good opportunity for Arnold to put some nice dollars in his pocket.

One busy day, Arnold's assistant tells him that they've run out of paper dishes. In those days, you couldn't just run out to Costco for more. This was a problem. There were still a lot more hungry fair visitors to feed and money to make. How would it look if he packed up and left mid-day? Plenty of other ice cream vendors would happily take his spot.

Right next to Arnold's stall, a man named Ernest was selling zalabi, a kind of crispy waffle treat. Ernest was a Syrian immigrant, and he had gotten to know Arnold over the time they'd both been working the fair. Arnold's plight inspired Ernest to come up with a solution that could save the day and make them both some money.

Roll up a waffle and put the ice cream in it.

It worked, of course, and the ice cream cone was a hit at the World's Fair. Ernest saved the day. Crisis averted. But even more than that, a whole new product, a new industry in fact, had accidentally been invented. Not long after, Ernest founded the Missouri Cone Company and became a cone tycoon. Soon, you could get an ice cream cone anywhere.

Like all good founding stories, there's a little bit of myth in this one. It was actually Italo Marchiony, an Italian immigrant, who invented the cone in 1896, eight years before the World's Fair. But it took this crisis to truly spread the idea. We eat ice cream cones by the ton today, but they wouldn't be so popular had Arnold never run out of dishes.

In 2020, the live entertainment industry started using waffles (online platforms) to serve their ice cream (shows). This novel idea got many organizations through a rough patch called the COVID-19 pandemic. But online events weren't actually new. The National Theatre in the UK, the Metropolitan Opera in New York, and others had been doing online shows for a decade. I invested in a small company in 2014 that enabled online shows and ticketing. Just like Marchiony, the company invented something that worked. But the crisis made the idea blow up.

Once ice cream cones took off, people never went back. But imagine they had. After all, people love ice cream and go through a lot to get it. After the crisis was over, ice cream sellers could have gone back to selling ice cream by the "penny lick." This was a truly disgusting but common practice in which ice cream was sold in something like a thick shot glass with a base. You bought it for a penny and then handed the glass back over to the seller, who may or may not wash it for the next customer. Cities often banned the penny lick because it spread tuberculosis and cholera. Truly vile. But it was a standard practice, a status quo way of doing things. Some people probably liked it. I bet somebody had a penny lick collection. Yuck.

Having survived the crisis, Arnold and Ernest knew they were onto something. The cone added something new to their world. A person could buy ice cream and take it with them. Ever walked through a park on a sunny day with an ice cream cone? Thank Marchiony, Arnold, and Ernest.

There are two kinds of live entertainment organizations postpandemic. One just wants to go back to the before-times. Believe me, I understand this. The other saw something else. They don't want to go back. They want to go forward. They are thrilled to have in-person events back, but they also want to put their new skills to work.

It's been a time of challenge, sacrifice, and uncertainty. These future-facing organizations see the silver lining of the very dark clouds of the pandemic. Online events offer an alternative to the Business Model of the Damned.

They're our ice cream cones.

Many of us have realized they can be more than a stopgap solution to a temporary problem. They can be a supercharger to the business of live events. They can create new opportunities to reach audiences, develop great work, and make more money. It's the one big win coming from a time of too much loss, and it's too important to miss.

In this section, you'll learn what you should produce if you don't want to miss out. We'll cover the three main kinds of online events and how to succeed with each of them.

CHAPTER 8

ONLINE-ONLY EVENTS

In March of 2020, the live events industry ran out of ice cream dishes...and ice cream too! If you were in the industry at the time, I bet you'll never forget the week that it...all...got...canceled. Tonight's show, tomorrow night's show, all next week's shows. The week after that, and, oh yes, the week after that, and...when exactly do we stop canceling?

We soon learned that the answer was "cancel everything." It made you feel like a wide-eyed comic-book character with the word "Gulp" over your head. There wasn't anything to do *except* cancel stuff. Cancellations-R-Us.

People are resilient, though. In just a matter of days, organizations and artists were doing shows, but they had moved them online. In the early days, they were simple—mostly over Zoom—with the camera pointed at someone's head and shoulders. These shows were not so much actual shows as acts of defiance in the face of death and fear. They let people know that the world hadn't ended. The goal was to cheer people up, keep them from going crazy. And for a short while, they were charming. It was kind of cool to see what kind of sofas your favorite musicians and actors have in their living rooms.

But the novelty wore off, as did the charm. You could forgive the low production value given the circumstances. But the content was pretty slapdash too. The content often felt thrown together, and that was because it was.

One well-known comedian did an "online show" from her living room. Fair enough. No venues were open. But she didn't have to stop periodically to take a bite of her lunch! Hard to imagine she'd do this onstage. The message was clear: this wasn't a "real" show. It was an online show.

As we've seen, some people's perceptions of online shows got stuck in that era. For them, "online show" and "Zoom show" mean the same thing. They're boring, low quality, and on software built for meetings. And the performer is usually on their sofa wearing a robe.

Then things started to change. Most of us, however, needed a little more time to catch on. A friend in the business asked me how much of this I thought would survive the pandemic, and I said, "Zero percent."

But in April and May of 2020, I started to see something new. At Goldstar, we were selling "online events" to support our partners and keep ourselves busy. Doing so gave us a window into what was happening and how customers were responding. I saw some artists putting more work into their shows and getting good results. Jeremy Wein in New York with his Play-Per-View shows upped the ante on acting quality. Hershey Felder with his one-man piano show on Mother's Day. That show, in particular, showed me the possibilities of the medium. It was well-filmed and beautifully performed. It used video effects, and Hershey even interacted live with the audience via text.

The "robe concerts" were still happening, but there was something else happening too: professional, live events people really wanted to see.

That's when it clicked for me. These were good shows worth watching and worth paying for. And that's what people were doing.

We began to imagine where online events could go from there, and the possibilities seemed limitless. We started building Stellar not long after that. We knew that for creators to thrive, they'd need more than a Zoom link, a password, and a Venmo account. They'd need the tools befitting creative professionals.

These professionals are doing some great online shows in a wide variety of genres. An incomplete list includes theatre, music, dance and other performing arts, magic and illusionist shows, comedy, talk and interview, cooking, film premieres, and even ice skating. But that's just the beginning. Anything you can put on a screen can be the basis of an online event.

Together, we were all pioneering a new medium. In this new medium, there were plenty of unknowns. Think back to 2007 at the launch of the iPhone. I bet you forgot there was no such thing as an app store then. The iPhone was in its early form, but it was easy to see the possibilities. The app store didn't come along for another year. You couldn't make an in-app purchase until 2009. It took time.

It's the same for online events. At the time I'm writing this, it's still early days. But we can already say a few things with confidence. No matter what kind of online event you're running, the following points hold true.

ONLINE EVENTS SHOULD BE DESIGNED FOR A SCREEN

First, an online event is designed to be watched *on a screen*. That seems basic, but it's essential to remember. A live, in-person event has to accommodate the physical viewpoint of everybody there. In actuality, the design goal is usually to provide an ideal view for the people in the best seats and an acceptable one for everyone else. Set and stage designers have to work with the physical constraints of the venue. Key parts of the action or set can't happen out of view of the audience, or people tend to get a little annoyed.

An online event doesn't have this particular problem. Everybody's "seat" can have the same view. You could deliberately make the view of the event worse for cheaper tickets. There's a sadistic minority out there who like to punish people for paying too little. Don't do this. More importantly, don't think like this. Thinking like this means you're really not doing an online event. You're just sticking a camera in front of an in-person event.

Early in the life of a new medium, this tends to happen. The transition from radio to TV was a huge change, and some radio shows struggled to really "get" video. Early TV is a bit awkward with the visual language it uses. To those of us raised on video for the last 60 years or so, early TV looks simplistic and a bit forced. It's easy to understand why. The challenge for the early TV pioneers was to leave the old medium behind (radio) and learn the new one. They had to develop new skills along with their old ones.

The challenge for online events creators is somewhat similar. You've got to create something optimized for a screen. Or, more accurately, any kind of screen. People may watch online events on a big television, a big computer screen, a laptop or tablet, or even a phone. Those aren't all the same, but creators have to think about them all.

For this reason, it's critical to have people on your team with film skills. You want to marry those skills with what you already know about making an event powerful and compelling.

Think of the attendee at an in-person event as the *director* of the show. They decide where the "camera" goes at any given moment. They point their eyes wherever they think it's likely to be the most important or interesting place to look. Of course, as a director, they're limited by the fact that they only have one camera (their eyes), and they can't really move it much because they're stuck in a seat.

For an online event, the creator of the show is in charge of choosing what exactly is on the screen. This is a serious responsibility. An online viewer can't swivel their head or look up or down, and their view is two dimensional. The good news is there's an entire, well-established art to this. Those early TV pioneers struggled at first, but they figured it out. Between camera movement and switching cameras, a good director can do a lot. They can create emotion and bring what's in front of the camera to life in amazing new ways.

Again, you need to have people on your team (if not you) who understand the filmmaking of it all. Today, you shouldn't have any trouble finding people with those skills. In fact, you have to!

Bad online events ignore this completely. They use a single camera shot and give no thought to the composition of that shot. Once or twice, someone asked me if I thought they could use their archival video[24] for an online show.

A teachable moment.

Watch your archival video, I said, and then tell me if you think someone would pay to see it.

That usually gets the point across. The archival video is a way to preserve what happened. It's a historical document. Online-event video is artistic, designed for people to watch. Of course, it does a pretty great job of recording the event for historical purposes too!

----

24 Archival video preserves a record of a show or performance. It's usually a broad shot with a single camera. It's not meant to be watched and enjoyed so much as to act as a "document" recording what happened. What's on stage may be great, but the purpose of archival video isn't the viewer's enjoyment.

Think of the differences between two audiobooks. In the first, the narrator reads in a very straightforward way. It's almost as if they're reading it for dictation. In the second, the narrator actually *performs* the book. The experience is completely different. You, of course, want to be like the latter. And the visual composition is critical to the performance. It shouldn't only be a faithful record of what happened.

These principles should affect all of your decisions. Set designers pay a lot of attention to the way things look for in-person events. In the same way, you will need to design specifically for a screen.

I can't predict exactly where online events will go, but this will remain true: your show has to look good on a screen.

ADVANTAGES OF ONLINE EVENTS OVER IN-PERSON EVENTS

There are at least three major advantages of an online event that do show up in the event itself: *access, participation, and community.*

By *access,* I mean the ability to put the audience anywhere you want them to be. You can point the cameras at the stage, but you can point them at other things too. You can be in the psyche-up circle just before the musicians run out on stage. You can follow a character down a hallway for some kind of important plot reveal. You can jump off the Hollywood sign in a paraglider. You could do anything and let the audience see it. This includes things that would be quite impossible for an in-person show.

Audiences love the feeling of access to the hidden or the surprising. Immersive theatre does this really well. I mentioned *Alma* before. During that show, I walked onto a bus that, to my surprise, started up and drove around the neighborhood. That doesn't happen every time you go to the theatre. The producers embedded this hidden surprise, and I still remember it vividly.

Online events make doing this kind of thing much, much easier. The question is where can you take the fan? What can you show them? The rules are unwritten at this point, so they're up for grabs. To date, in my opinion, online event producers are under-doing this advantage by miles, but that won't last forever. People will innovate, and the successful innovators will reap some big rewards.

It doesn't even have to be all that grand in scope. Imagine, for example, that there's something in a briefcase that's critical to a story. An in-person event will just gloss over this or show the people in the first row. It's a mystery to the rest of us.[25]

With an online event, you can reveal the contents in a bunch of creative and exciting ways. You could use an over-the-shoulder camera, a flyover camera, a point-of-view camera worn by one of the characters, or something else. The point is not the technology. The point is that, if you want, you've got new ways to add color and texture to the plot. You can improve the watcher's experience *because* you're working in an online medium. That's true *access*. Allowing people to see, hear, and be a part of your world. Possibly in ways that are impossible in the physical world.

Along with *access*, online events create the possibility of *participation*. In-person events have participation too, but it's pretty limited. In the best of cases, even at a fully immersive event like *Sleep No More*, you can't do much. If you haven't been, *Sleep No More* opened in New York City in 2011. It's a show that's happening all around you, and you choose which part to watch. It covers an enormous multi-story space made to look like an old-fashioned hotel, and you decide what part to watch and when. But, you only have so much power. You can basically move around, deciding what

---

25 And not in a good way, like the deliberately mysterious briefcase in the movie *Pulp Fiction*.

you want to passively watch. On rare occasions, one or two patrons may have a brief encounter with a cast member, but that's all.

Cirque du Soleil works hard to create the illusion that an audience member is participating. If somebody from the crowd ends up high diving into a tiny pool of water during *O*, they're not a civilian. They're a highly trained performer! Think about that. Just the idea of an audience member participating is thrilling. Cirque gets it. Online events make participation much easier.

What do you think of when you hear the term "audience participation"? The answer is different for different people. Some people hate it. They don't want to be singled out or embarrassed, and who can blame them? For other people, it's a chance to be a big ham. You know at least one person like that, I'm sure. Audience participation makes me think of corny attempts to talk to someone who wants to sit down. Unless it's done well, these moments are often just dead spots in the show. Sometimes, the moments are built in so the crew can set for the next scene.

Online shows open up entire new possibilities here. In the summer of 2020, the illusionist Helder Guimaraes did this to perfection. In a hit online show called *The Present*, all 24 different patrons each night were critical to the action. Beforehand, you received a little mysterious box in the mail. In this box, you found everything you needed to play along with what Helder did. Without the audience, there was no show. He was the perfect master of ceremonies, but the audience was where the action was.

This is just the beginning, and there's no limit. But it's going to need some innovation. Is an in-person concert participatory? In a way, it is: the band plays and the audience cheers. Interaction! The lead singer says it's great to be in Cleveland (or wherever), and people go crazy. Interaction! But mainly, you listen, you cheer, you leave.

There's nothing wrong with this. It works. I wouldn't advocate for in-person events to add much to the mix. The live, in-person event's strength is absorption, being there, getting swept up. You don't need to be fiddling on the phone when you're there.

But with online events, there's a lot more room for active engagement. In fact, you need to create participation in an online event, even if it's just chat and emoji-based cheering. People watching need to see and feel the presence of others. But it doesn't have to stop there. It's going to be exciting to see how participation evolves. It's one of the native strengths of online events, and it leads into the third strength: *community*.

Almost 20,000 people watched the *Jagged Live in NYC*: A Broadway Reunion Concert on Stellar in December of 2020. The concert was wonderful, and the audience loved it. But what happened after the show was powerful too. More than a thousand people stayed in the chat for an hour after the final curtain. There was nothing left to do but talk to the other people there. They talked about the show, of course. And they talked about where they were all from, and then...they just kept talking!

This wasn't just *participation*. This was something more: *community*. Let's face it. With an in person event, it's hard to achieve community. Most of the time, people come in, sit in their seats, and leave. At a baseball game, you might high-five the person next to you when your team hits a home run. But do you talk to them? It's rare.

Even rarer is building some kind of bond or relationship with other attendees. The Fab Four is the world's best Beatles tribute band. They were also one of the first artists to use Stellar back in the summer of 2020. They've been around almost 25 years, and they're really good. Most of that time, of course, they've been touring the world and accumulating fans. The pandemic and the advent of online events created a new way for those fans to get to know each other.

In the Stellar chat.

Whole books have been written about building community online, but online events are a whole new way for people to come together. The intensity of live events and the reach and accessibility of the internet is a powerful mix.

If your online events can create moments of community for people, I don't see how you can fail. It's rare enough today for people to have a community of any kind. In modern society, many people feel more alone than ever. This hard truth makes community more valuable to people. Online events can give people a sense of belonging and togetherness, even when they're scattered around the world. This is powerful stuff!

In the future, there will be online events with so many participants it will puzzle some people. So many people will be paying money to attend so often that others will say the whole thing is stupid. They'll say this because they don't understand the power of community. Think of services like Twitch, where people gather for live "events." Though these are generally free to watch and the content is more spontaneous, they still come. Do the fans find it entertaining? Sure, they do, but they also like being there watching with others. The same will be true for high-value content that people pay for.

Eventually, the numbers will be stunning and "unexplainable." Some will roll their eyes at the whole thing. They'll call it names because they feel secretly threatened and out of touch. Ignore those people.

Instead, use the three inherent strengths of online events to your advantage and succeed.

Let's review. *Access.* This is the ability to show the audience things you couldn't show them in real life. You can put them in places that would be impossible in a venue. *Participation.* This is the ability of the audience to take part in the show. *Community.*

This is creating a sense of connection and belonging with other people during the event.

No matter what happens, an online event creator will have these to work with. How creators use them will evolve and improve. Eventually, no online event will be complete without them.

SHOULD YOU DO AN ONLINE-ONLY EVENT?

During the pandemic, all online events were online only. Post-pandemic, creators have more options. Still, there could be reasons for a show to be online only, even if you can host an audience in person.

First, the presence of a physical audience may be unnecessary or even a negative. Take, for example, the British online audio-only event *Darkfield*. It is a very personal experience. Other people might actually distract you from enjoying it.

Second, hosting an audience is expensive! There's venue rental and security. There are costs to do in-person ticketing. Craft services and equipment rentals. Of course, the audience is also a revenue source, but that's a big tradeoff you have to weigh.

If you think the audience is a drawback or not worth it, maybe an online-only event is right for you. Online-only is certainly a viable choice. Trust your instincts, and see how the numbers look. You might be right.

AVOIDING RADIO ON TELEVISION

Let's talk about one of the main pitfalls to avoid with online events. It's what I call "radio on TV." Some early TV shows were holdovers from the age of radio. *Gunsmoke*, *Superman*, *Ozzy and Harriet*, *Dragnet*, and *I Love Lucy* succeeded on the screen. Others didn't make the leap because, unlike the shows I just mentioned, they were doing radio on TV. They didn't adapt. Producers didn't play to the new medium's strengths, instead transplanting what they did on radio to television.

By contrast, watch the famous "chocolate factory" scene from a 1952 episode of *I Love Lucy*. It's very early in the history of TV, and you can see Lucille Ball taking full advantage of the new medium. This scene wouldn't even make sense on radio, but it's a scream on TV. Lucy and Ethel are working in a chocolate factory and sitting at a conveyor belt. Their job is to wrap each chocolate that comes out of the last workstation and replace it on the belt. Then, each piece goes through a slot in the wall to the next workstation. At first, all is well, but the belt keeps speeding up. Lucy and Ethel go from confident to frantic. They resort to all kinds of idiotic "solutions" to their problems. They eat some. They hide them in their hats and stuff them down their shirts. It's hysterical.

By the way, a written explanation of the scene, like the one I just wrote, is akin to radio on TV too. It's an accurate description of the scene but completely lifeless. You may understand what happened, and maybe it made you want to see the actual scene. But compared to seeing it on video, it's totally lame. That's how it feels when the medium and communication style are not aligned.

Remember: online events aren't just in-person events with a camera pointed at them. They're a new medium, with strengths and limitations. Don't be *radio on TV*.

To make online events work, you must commit to learning what's effective in this medium. But don't worry. We're all learning together.

LEARN FAST BY CHALLENGING YOUR ASSUMPTIONS

One way to start learning is to drop your assumptions about how live events should be run. Here are a few questions you might ask.

How long should a show be? Most in-person shows are between 90 minutes and two and a half hours. Is that right for the online-event world? Things could change, but for now, you should err on the shorter side. Ninety minutes is a good target.

What can you do with audio? You have more control of your audio with online events. What can you do with that? I mentioned *Darkfield*, an audio-only, ticketed, online event. They push audio to the max! There's an opportunity to use audio in novel ways along with video, so if you're inspired, go for it.

Speaking of video, you can and should do a lot with *cameras and camera angles*. If you can shoot with two or three cameras, do it. But that's only table stakes. What if you had 10 cameras? You can tell a whole different story that way.

What other assumptions from producing in-person events are you carrying over? No, you don't need to change everything, but it's worth turning over those rocks and seeing what's there. Innovation in a new medium involves a lot of trying, most of which doesn't get you very far, but sometimes, it does!

In fact, at this stage, a small tweak can create an explosion of growth. Think of how Apple added a GPS chip to the iPhone 3G in 2008. A year later, Uber was founded. Most people saw GPS as a tool for getting directions or navigating in the wilderness. Uber questioned that assumption and invented a whole new type of business for location-based services. That in turn had a massive impact on the way people live. In retrospect, the innovation seems obvious, but it wasn't at the time. Uber had to turn over those rocks to find something interesting.

Be willing to reconsider everything, but take things one step at a time. You don't have to do it all at once. The process is more evolutionary. If we do this right, next year's online-event content will be better than this year's. And a few years from now, today's shows might even seem a little embarrassing. That's not a bad thing. It's a sign of a new medium, a new industry, being born.

Consider the pioneering websites of 1995 or 1996. Amazon made secure online purchasing possible. Ebay created the notion of an "online auction." Those companies and literally a million others brought the consumer internet into being, one step at a time. Sometimes, those steps weren't pretty. But by '99, companies were making elegant, functional websites that made their old sites look like ransom notes.

Online events will change, but the change will happen one step at a time. But if we zoom out a bit, the change will actually happen rapidly. Just as it did with the internet in the '90s. It's exciting to be part of something new!

What won't change for online events? The content will always need to be worth the viewer's time. Again, you can't skimp on *quality*. There's no free pass just because it's on a computer screen. If anything, the quality should be higher because an online viewer is more distractible.

Likewise, *service* still makes or breaks the experience. In a venue or online, people have questions, problems, and needs. A friendly, knowledgeable voice has to be there to step in and make everything work. In fact, the entire *experience* is crucial.

It's worth asking the following questions before you go live: Is it easy to get into my online show? Can it be watched on any internet-connected device? Are the controls easy to find, understand, and use? Does it look good? Does it feel good?

Remember that people still bring their peopleness to an online show. It's up to you to make sure you meet them with humanity of your own.

THINGS YOU CAN DO WITH ONLINE EVENTS

Once you've got the knack for successful online events, you've really got something. That's because you can achieve a lot of different goals through this new medium.

If you just want to *make money and do a great show*, that's possible. You can contain costs, and if you get the content right, you can sell an unlimited number of tickets and make real money. But there are other, more specific ways to put these events to use.

As a *development platform*, online events are great. Early in the life of a new show, the online format is a relatively cheap way to get a real audience's response. It's easier to survey an online audience, and you can get a lot of data. When did people stop watching? When did they get excited in chat or with the reaction emojis?

We learned in early 2021 that Stellar could be a path to future success for theatre shows. Producers could bring a new concept with a big future to the screen first. *Titanique* debuted in May of that year, and it was a hit on Stellar. The goals for the show are ambitious, including bigger and bigger stages, touring, and who knows what else. Fingers crossed for *Titanique*. Whatever happens with that show, the online format will be invaluable for developing content and seeing what works.

Online events can also be a great *marketing tool*. You can create an audience you can use again or for something else. The Geffen "Stayhouse" in Los Angeles was a pandemic-era star. It produced great online shows, but that wasn't all. It not only charged up its regular audience, it built a brand new one.

While most were fighting to remain relevant, Geffen was growing. It added people by the tens of thousands to its list of fans. Josh Groban, the musician, did the same thing. He was one of the first big pop acts to create fully realized concerts online. Sure, he made big sales, but he also earned the attention of music fans he didn't have before.

While a lot of musicians sat on their sofas, Josh was winning over thousands of new people.

Oh, and making money in the process. It's a marketing program that pays you.

Online events can be an excellent way of *fundraising* for a nonprofit or cause. The Smuin Contemporary Ballet Company in San Francisco provides a great example of this. The year 2020 was an existential challenge for them, just as it was for so many nonprofits, but Smuin adapted.

It changed the content of its shows. Individual performers took a role in the creation of it, and people followed those performers online. By the holidays, Smuin was ready to do its major fundraising event of the year, and it was a runaway success. They demolished every goal they set and raised more money than ever before in a holiday event.

I can't promise that will happen to you. But let's think about why it happened to them. Fundraising is important for nonprofits, but it might not be a top priority for patrons. If they like an organization or cause, they might be willing to support it financially, but they aren't always willing to go out of their way to do this. Online events actually make it easier for people to give. No travel, no babysitter, no dressing up needed.

If it's easier, more people will probably participate. They might even feel more generous because of the money they've saved.

Platforms like Stellar make donating almost effortless. It's much easier to click a button on a screen than to write a check and mail it in. And as time goes on, it's only going to get easier and smoother. Don't miss out if you're a nonprofit or cause marketer.

You can use online events for *subscriber retention or rewards* too. You can run a special online event that only donors and supporters can see or join, giving them a good reason to keep the donations coming in.

For organizations with geographically dispersed supporters, the benefits of online events just get bigger.

SUCCESS DOESN'T SUCK

The main reason to do an online event, of course, is the same reason you do any event.

Did you think I was going to say "money"?

Sure, everybody's got to make a living. That's a given. And of course, everybody would like to make a fortune.

But very few people in this business do it for the money alone. Very few musicians or even music managers would enjoy being accountants. Even if the money was the same or better, most wouldn't switch.

The "why" for most theatre people sure isn't the moolah. Not that you can't make a good living at it. You can. But this industry can be tough too.

Lots of people who work in live entertainment scrape by, even ones that have success and do good work. That's part of the reality, I suppose. They love the work and hope the money comes along. Sometimes it does, but sometimes it doesn't.

Beyond money, online events represent another path. The new medium offers a bigger stage on which to do the work you want to do. An artist or an organization can take control. They can skip the gatekeepers.

There's a worldwide platform with unlimited scale at your fingertips if you can figure out how to use it. And if you do, you can be a huge success.

If that sounds good to you, it's time to devote serious time and effort to mastering the online-only event.

In the next chapter, we'll cover hybrid events, which combine an in-person event with an online event. I'm a huge fan. There's gigantic potential here too.

Keep reading so you can decide which doors you want to walk through!

CHAPTER 9

HYBRID EVENTS

Anakin Skywalker, George W. Bush, a *Teenage Mutant Ninja Turtles* villain, and Gaston from *Beauty and the Beast* said it.

Dirty Harry, Mussolini, *Survivor* contestants, and characters from *Ben-Hur* and *The Crucible* also said it.

"You're either with me, or you're against me."

Sometimes, it's an easy choice. I'm *contro* you, Mussolini.[26]

But usually, it's trickier. People say this to create a *false dilemma*—a "fallacy that erroneously limits what options are available." In other words, if I can make you think you've got only two choices, I can make you do what I want.

Are you in favor of raising the budget for the animal shelters, or are you a puppy murderer?

Do you want to take the job I'm offering you and be happy or turn it down and be miserable?

Do you like electronic dance music, or are you old and out of touch?

Do you want to support in-person events or go with online events and kill the in-person experience until in-person events are gone forever?

---

26 Easy for me to say now, I suppose. Harder under fascist control.

This is a classic false dilemma. It's a result of completely unnecessary either/or thinking combined with a little bit of fear. That's okay. I understand. We're going to work through that.

The COVID-19 pandemic hit the live industry like an 18-wheeler driving through a tent. It was a traumatic time, and in that time, online events took off.

Because of this dynamic, people sometimes see online events as a substitute for in-person events. But now that "the real thing" is back, we don't need the substitute.

Understandable, but wrong. Remember: Online events aren't a stopgap. They're a supercharger!

If you're reading this *not* during a pandemic, you're lucky! You can choose whether to charge people to come to a place and watch a show. It's a fun thing to do, and people are willing to pay to come, so you should do it.

The next time you have one of these in-person events, take a moment and look around. Whether you're in a small club or a theater or an arena or a stadium, look at the people. Try to look at as many of them as you can. Scan across the sections of seats. See them not as different-colored blobs filling sections but as individual people. See them in your mind's eye right now, the people.

No matter how big the venue is, you'll have no trouble imagining all the people, as John Lennon said. There they are, right in front of you. Now stop and think about the fact that no matter how many people you're looking at right now, there are so many more.

In fact, try to imagine how many more there are. Picture a river with a big grass field on each side. On the left of the river, put all the people you saw in the event. See them sitting there having a picnic. Got it?

Now on the right side of the river, picture first all the people living within a mile of the venue. No matter the number, picture them.

Now imagine all the people living within 10 miles of the venue. If you're in New York, the group's already enormous! This is an epic picnic for the ages, and it makes the group on the left—the ones in the venue—look scant in number.

But keep zooming out in whatever size steps you want to go. Put all those people to the right of the river, and keep your venue people on the left. They start to look like a rather paltry band, even if you started with a full crowd at Dodger Stadium.

Stop and dwell on the moment. See how big the crowd on the right is? It's astounding, don't you think? How many of them might want to see what the people on the left were seeing in the venue?

Hybrid events make it possible for the big group to join in.

With a hybrid event, you don't have to choose a side. You can have *both*.

The false dilemma in online events is that it's either online events or in-person events. That's some pretty lousy either/or thinking. You can do both, and with a hybrid event, you can do both at the same time.

RIDE-ALONG HYBRID EVENTS

Let's start by talking about the two basic types of hybrid events. The first, and the most common, type is what I call a *ride-along event*. This is an in-person event that the producer also films and broadcasts for an online audience. Imagine a live concert that you can also watch online. Or the premiere of a new Broadway musical or a big comic's performance on the Las Vegas strip. Of course, it's not limited to shows like this. A hybrid event can be anything. My theoretical Greatest Small Theatre in the World will be doing hybrid events too.

Everyone in the industry will be able to do these.

Plus, you'll like the way the budgets look for these events. Assume that the in-person event has a budget and P&L that makes basic sense. You're already doing the show, so presumably you have a chance to make your money back. As discussed, the costs of the online part of the show don't add all that much. This is especially true once you've got a venue wired and equipped with cameras and sound equipment.

Remember the Business Model of the Damned? This is how you get out of that for good.

And if that doesn't move you, you'll be reaching way more people. For a musician or other artist, hybrid events build and strengthen your fanbase. In the performing arts and nonprofit worlds, access matters. This is the best opportunity ever to make access a here-and-now reality.

In fact, I'll go further than that. If you talk about "access" but don't add online events to your current in-person events, you're not serious about access.

The ride-along hybrid event is a no-brainer, really. Sports on TV should be the only example you need to see the power of it. Do you think it helps or hurts the NBA that you can go to the game or watch the game on TV? The formula for success in live sports is a little different, but it's just a matter of figuring it out.

Ride-along hybrid events are a good investment. Here are a few things to help succeed with these.

Do the filming right. People watching online are watching through the lens you're giving them. It's important to give them something great. We talked about this in Chapter 8 if you want more detail. You need a director who can make good use of more than one camera. You want titles and pre-show content. This isn't a webcam pointed at a street corner. It's a show!

Make the online audience first-class citizens. It's exciting to be at an in-person event and know that lots of other people are watching around the world! Your in-person customer won't feel slighted by the fact that there's an online audience. If anything, they feel good about it. They're in a place that's so cool it's worth watching from home. Mention the online audience from the stage during the event. Think of them as audience members right alongside the ones in the building. Don't do anything to make the online viewer feel like a second-class citizen. They shouldn't be punished just because they're not there. You might even take a moment to have the assembled crowd wave to the at-home crowd! Include them in key moments if you can. It will pay off.

Don't geofence if you don't have to. Geofencing is technically limiting the availability of a show to exclude certain areas. It's like putting a metaphorical fence around an area and stopping the people there from being able to see it.

The best way for me to explain why you shouldn't geofence is with a story.

One of the least effective and most unpopular moves in the history of sports was the NFL's blackout policies. For years, local audiences were "punished" by their NFL team for not selling out the stadium each game. NFL rules didn't allow broadcasting the game on TV in the local market if ticket sales weren't good enough.

If ever a nose was cut off to spite a face in the world of event marketing, this was it. If an NFL team wasn't particularly good, or if, in fact, it stunk to high heaven, in-person attendance would naturally wane. And then the games got blacked out.

Did blacking out an unpopular team help rebuild support?

What do you think?

Why the NFL thought that it should punish the fans because the team was terrible, I have no idea.

As Yogi Berra said, "If people don't want to come out to the ballpark, nobody's gonna stop 'em." Attendance dropped, so the games disappeared from TV. Fewer people followed the teams, so selling out the games became more challenging. It became difficult for some teams to recover. Why? Because fewer people cared at all anymore.

You can't "punish" people by taking something away they don't want. Over time, these policies eased. The league started making "exceptions," and the blackout was "suspended" in 2016. Give the league some credit. They had a chance to undo the most foolish thing they ever did, so they took it. They've continued to "suspend" the blackout rule each year since then too.

I share this story because it's a good illustration of why you should avoid geofencing. I hear two suggestions for geofencing. Make the event available *everywhere except* **the market** in which it's happening. Or make the event available *only* **in the market** in which it's happening.

With rare exceptions, they're both bad ideas. Let's knock 'em down one at a time.

The first is a remix of the NFL's worst idea: *nobody near my venue can watch* the online version of the event. For example, a theatre in New York "blacks out" the New York metro area. This is to "make" people show up at the venue. Again, this is a truly terrible idea. Why? For starters, it eliminates your strongest market for online sales. That limits your reach where it matters most. It turns off the flow of awareness-building that the online event can provide. You lose most of the financial benefits of doing a hybrid event and stop your audience growth.

It also shows a lack of confidence in the value of the in-person experience. Are people only there because it's the only way they can see your show? I don't think so.

You can generally tell an idea is bad when you're "punishing" your customers. You're on the wrong track when you think customers are doing things the wrong way. The NFL came up with this policy in 1973, and that's where it belongs.

The second form is not as bad. This is when *only people near my venue* can watch the event online. For example, for an LA concert, the whole world except LA is blacked out for the show. The purpose is to create a "virtual tour." The idea is to replicate a tour by moving the geofence around as the act goes from city to city. What's good about this is that local promoters can flex their marketing muscles. They can reach a local audience for a show that's happening in a familiar location.

Still, doing this eliminates virtually the entire world as an audience. It resurrects the Business Model of the Damned. Local promoters have a lot of value to add to the marketing of online events. Getting them involved and paid is a great idea. But the best way to do that is not by replicating a physical tour with a virtual one.

Instead, pick a few dates from the tour and make those your online concerts. Give local promoters a shot to promote all of them. They can tap their local audiences for sales and even double-dip. Locations late in the tour can build a list of online buyers and hit them up for in-person tickets later. Locations early in the tour can sell in-person tickets but then keep selling once those are sold out. If someone missed the chance to see it in person, they might want to catch it online.

Cannibalization is less of a worry than you think. Fans are fans. Those who buy something tend to be most likely to buy more of that thing. You never want to get in the way of that.

Online events make geofencing possible, but there aren't many good reasons to do it. International licensing might be one of the few. Block people in some countries to avoid getting sued by a mega-corporation. That sounds like a good idea. Blocking people in New Jersey to "make them" drive to Philly does not.

Cross market to both audiences. Your in-person buyers might want to see their show again online. Your online buyer might be free the next time you've got this show in your venue. Your online buyers are great prospects for in-person tickets and vice versa. Why? Because when people like something, they tend to want more. Amazon has been tweaking its recommendation algorithm for 20 years. Still, most of the time, it suggests that you buy something very, very similar to things you already bought. You liked the book *Gone Girl?* Try *Sharp Objects* by the same author, Gillian Flynn. You liked *The Stand* by Stephen King? You might also like *Cell* because that's also about the end of the world.

It's the same idea here. Online show buyers are in-person show buyers and vice versa. There are exceptions, of course. People who have health or mobility limitations that keep them at home may be unable to come to the venue. But overall, the audience for one is a very rich target for the other.

What should you do instead? Give every ticket buyer a free or very cheap video on-demand (VOD) add-on to their in-person ticket. Find ways to sell an in-person ticket along with every online buyer's purchase. You can also do this after the show, when everybody's basking in the glow of having a great time. Either way, nobody's going to feel spammed by this tactic if it's done right because it's relevant to them.

You can use all this information for ongoing marketing. It's the perfect opportunity to expand your permission with the buyers. For example, you might offer the VOD or a future online ticket in exchange for joining a mailing list or even a fan club. There are a million ways to do it, but do it. Hybrid events give you another way to connect with people. You've got another thing to sell them, another thing to talk to them about, and another thing to give them.

If you use them right, ride-along hybrid events will rain down gifts and goodness on you for years. Who'd want to miss that?

THE ONLINE-FIRST HYBRID EVENT

The second kind of hybrid event is what I call the *online-first event*. There's an audience in attendance, but the event has been designed for the online medium first. This is a cousin to the TV show filmed in front of a live audience. It's a great experience for a small number of live attendees, but the real point is the at-home audience.

The in-person audience is often part of the show. Their presence brings energy, laughter, applause, moments of surprise, and interaction. They will even be on camera sometimes. A good comparison is a late-night show or a game show. Viewers at home see the audience participating in more ways than just applauding. Think *The Tonight Show Starring Jimmy Fallon* or *The Price Is Right*.

These events combine a great at-home show with an exclusive, coveted, in-person experience. Maybe only a couple of hundred people are there in person. It doesn't matter if the crowd isn't enormous. The people in the room feel special. Late-night tickets are generally free but difficult to get. Tourists stand in long, inconvenient lines, and locals call in favors from friends to get them. It feels special to be there.

Live-entertainment producers have the skills to do these events even better. TV producers tend to treat the live audience like an afterthought or, even worse, as props. I'm not saying they don't care about the audience. They just see the world differently than those in the live business do when it comes to the guests in the building.

I love this kind of hybrid event because it's got unlimited potential. You could bring something very different to the world this way. Online events thrive, as we've said, based on access, participation, and community. Online-first events can do that in a very special way.

The in-person audiences for these will be smaller than for ride-along hybrid events. But they can become more a part of the show itself. I mentioned the late-night shows and how their audiences create atmosphere, but that's just a start. Late-night shows still usually keep their audiences off camera and seated in rows. You could take a different approach and create a whole vibe. There are endless possibilities.

In 1969 to 1970, there was a show called *Playboy After Dark*. Totally sfw, they shot the show in Hugh Hefner's "apartment." Watch it on YouTube sometime, and you'll see that they created a great live vibe, even though people watched on TV. Be warned if you do watch it, it's dated in ways that you can't ignore, but you can still learn something from it. The audience is very literally part of the show. The camera moves around inside the apartment, as opposed to being pointed at a stage. It goes from musical performances to conversations with famous authors with minimal friction. Then it's a poetry reading, and then all of a sudden, Tina Turner is singing over by the bookcase. The camera stands in for the viewer, moving around the space. You always have the best view of what's going on, but the in-person audience is there and having a great time. In today's terms, being there is the VIP ticket and a unique experience. But the online audience is the focus.

Online-first events also work well as recurring events or an ongoing performance series. These shows can run indefinitely. The content would change, but the format, the host, the location, the vibe, and so forth would not. People would attend and tune in for what the show's brand represents instead of the exact content.

The opportunity is big because it combines things that tend to work well. It combines the power of a special, live event and the comfort of the familiar. Big, special events come along, and they have a natural appeal. Big fights, new shows, or even breaking news—they pull people in. People love novelty. It's not hard to market the new. When I was in the restaurant business years and years ago, we used the same tactic. We'd concoct some new product and use that to get people back in the restaurant. It's called "new product news," and it works.

But people like familiarity too. For the UFC and WWE, each big event is also just another chapter in something its fans already know. WWE's big event is called *Wrestlemania*, and it's on series number 37. Hundreds of thousands of people still pay an average of about $45 to watch the event. UFC has taken a similar strategy, now on UFC 261. It's designed to be a habit, to be something that a viewer wants to return to.

Even if you don't like wrestling or ultimate fighting, you can see the applicability of the model. Create an "event." Give it uniqueness, specialness. Give it a feeling or a vibe—its own "brand."

Then, repeat it at the right interval, varying what makes it unique but keeping what makes it familiar.

Of all the forms we've discussed, this is one with the most flexibility and business potential. It's easy to imagine a recurring, popular show growing from online to a streaming service to spin-offs to tours and beyond. Somebody is going to get very famous and make a lot of money on these kinds of events, and it might as well be you.

REVIEW

So to recap, we've got the ride-along hybrid and the online-first hybrid. Both are great. I've found that everyone understands the ride-along concept. It's what you're doing now plus some cameras.

It takes most people a minute to grasp the online-first hybrid, but everyone sees the opportunity eventually. It's like one of those

Magic Eye pictures. At first, you see a wavy, blue blob, but if you keep staring, it's actually a friendly dolphin. Everyone can see it if they concentrate for a minute.

But imagine a Magic Eye picture that only one in 10,000 could see. No matter how much you stared at it, how fervently you crossed your eyes, it didn't stop being a blue blob. And you could pass it around the room, and no one else could see it either. You'd probably just put it down and forget about it. You might feel a little annoyed and say it was stupid. I wouldn't blame you.

There's a type of online event that I'm going to discuss next that's lurking in that wavy, blue blob. It's something that almost nobody can see right now.

As soon as the right person picks it up, though, they'll see it. Then they'll tell us what it is.

And then we'll see it.

We can't see what the future holds. Our perspective on what these events can be is clouded. But I believe what's coming around the corner will be breathtaking.

The biggest changes will drive the culture and generate the dollars. Somebody will see them and make them a reality. Once they do, it will all seem obvious to us in retrospect.

I call these events Wild Card events, and I'll talk about them in the next chapter.

CHAPTER 10

THE WILD CARD

In 1987, Guy faced a big decision and a big risk. His Canadian performing arts organization had been on a pretty good roll. It had been building its reputation and growing its crowds for the last two or three years. This earned it an invitation to open the Los Angeles Festival, thousands of miles away. Success there would mean bigger crowds and ticket sales. It could also lead to a much bigger profile in showbiz. Influential industry people would be there looking for what's coming up next. In other words, it was everything he and his group wanted and needed.

That's if they succeeded. If the crowds showed up, if they were a hit, Los Angeles would open a lot of doors for them. But if they didn't?

In poker terms, to take this risk, Guy would have to go "all-in." If the crowds stayed away, if they weren't a hit, they were going to run out of money. It would be a big expense for a small organization to make a trip like this. If they flopped, everybody and all the gear were going to be stuck in America. If his bet failed, he wouldn't even have the money to get them all home.

Well, he made the bet, and they were a hit. Such a hit that the *LA Times* wrote that Cirque du Soleil had "reinvented" the circus.[27]

Guy Laliberté and his other co-conspirators who founded Cirque du Soleil had created something new. Within a few years of that high-risk trip to LA, they had made the old and already shaky circus industry obsolete. In time, they built a performing arts empire unlike anything else in the world.

Cirque du Soleil was a Wild Card. It came out of nowhere and changed the circus world, but it did far more than that. It became a juggernaut of creativity, ticket sales, and artistic influence. It borrowed from the traditions of the circus and made something relevant to a new century. It delighted millions of people and helped bring animal acts in circuses to an end. The Wild Card won the whole game.

This story shows the power of something that reaches beyond traditional forms. The right Wild Card can shake up and transform long-static industries in a shockingly short period of time. Sometimes, they come from creative minds with a slightly odd bent to them. Guy and his team had always seen the world in a slightly cock-eyed, delightful way. Often though, these major shifts come from new technologies and the new capabilities they bring. Even more often, they come from combining those new capabilities with an audience looking for something new.

If the emergence of online events is a game of cards, you should know that there are some Wild Cards in the deck.

- - - - - - - - - - -

27 Dan Sullivan, "LE CIRQUE DU SOLEIL: SOMETHING NEW UNDER THE SUN: New-Wave, Old-Style, French-Canadian Troupe Opens Los Angeles Festival with a Circus That 'Reinvents' the Real Thing," Los Angeles Times, September 5, 1987, https://www.latimes.com/archives/la-xpm-1987-09-05-ca-1547-story.html.

In poker, a wild card is a card that can be anything. If "deuces are wild," then a player can use a two card as anything, however it is most advantageous. Similarly, the innovations that online events are bringing could be used in completely new ways, and somebody is going to play these cards.

Cirque du Soleil was a Wild Card of its own in the circus business. It eliminated the animals, raised the prices, and reclaimed old-time circus traditions. It got rid of scary, weird clowns and brought back fun ones. Its shows were fun for adults as well as children. The formula worked. It was packing its big top while the rest of the industry was in decline. Traditional circuses like Ringling Bros. were already trending down by the time Cirque came along. But with the new entrant, they looked even worse by comparison.

Of course, the old guard adjusted, but it hardly mattered. Within just a few years, Cirque was the most valuable "circus" property in the world.

Crushing the competition was for starters. Cirque du Soleil became more valuable than anybody thought a circus could be.

That's what happens when a Wild Card gets played. And in my strong opinion, the new medium of online events is dealing a fresh deck. We're going to see a few new Wild Cards, even if we don't yet know what they are.

Let's be specific. What is a Wild Card and how will we recognize it when we see it?

THREE QUALITIES OF A WILD CARD

Wild Cards have three qualities:

- They seem to *come out of nowhere*.

- They redefine *what's possible* in their genre or event category.

- They create an *avalanche of value*.

Of course, they only *seem* to **come out of nowhere**. In fact, they're the result of a lot of hard work. This work is often done quietly or away from the limelight. Guy and the Cirque gang had been getting good at this circus-without-animals thing for years. They were the biggest hit on the streets of Old Montreal. But then they would invade small towns in Quebec with their clown-and-acrobat army. They'd make a big impression and vanish back to the city. Their success didn't really happen overnight, but to the big shots in LA who saw them for the first time in 1987, it sure seemed like it did.

A Wild Card **redefines what's possible**. That's because they don't start with the same set of rules as the conventional winners do. The "leader" in the circus world "knew" that a circus needs an elephant, and I suppose at one point it did. Or at least, that was the set of rules to which everybody subscribed, except Cirque du Soleil. This is why the Wild Card rarely emerges from an existing leader. Because even when a leader tries very hard, the leader is still unconsciously beholden to a lot of rules. Some of those rules are the fruit of good experience, and some are simply relics. When an important rule-break occurs, new possibilities emerge. And that's what happens when someone plays a Wild Card.

Let's not forget the **avalanche of value**. It's what distinguishes things that are avant-garde or just weird from a Wild Card. There will always be rule-breakers learning their craft in obscurity. But if it stays obscure, it doesn't change much. When the Wild Card connects with a latent need or want that a lot of people have, it triggers the avalanche. People wanted a circus, but the arena-based circuses of the '70s and '80s were dull, dated, and tacky. The clowns were the stuff of nightmares, and everybody knew it except Ringling Bros.

But Cirque knew from experience there was something *else* people wanted. It got what a circus was all about and knew it could give it to people.

Cirque seemed to come from nowhere, redefined what was possible, and created an avalanche of value. Exciting, right?

Wild Cards are in the deck now in a whole new way with online events. What might happen? I would bet that the biggest live entertainment organization in five years does not exist or is embryonic today. Wherever and whoever they may be, they will crack the code for online events. They'll create something astonishingly new and trigger that avalanche.

Or one of today's leaders will make that jump. If that happens, they'll extend their leadership and ensure success for a generation. Most of the leading organizations in the live world are at least paying lip service to online events right now, but who will step out and truly change the game? Time will tell.

BERRIED IN APPLES

Wild Cards mean one thing to you if you're Ringling Bros. and another if you're Cirque du Soleil. Which one is your organization? Of course, nobody wants to be Ringling Bros. in this example, so I'll change it to something a little easier to swallow.

Wild Cards mean one thing to you if you're Blackberry in 2007 and another if you're Apple in 2007.

If you're Blackberry in 2007, you're the biggest name in smartphones. You've got nearly 10 percent of the global smartphone market and 100 percent of the cool factor. You're a generic term. You're an addiction (during this time, the common term was "crackberry"). More and more, people are adopting smartphones, so you're growing like crazy.

If you're Apple in 2007, you're about to release the iPhone. You have 0 percent of the worldwide market, and nobody thinks of you as a "phone" company. What you believe you do have, though, is a Wild Card. It's a completely different idea of what a phone is. It's got a touchable interface, and it looks like a space rock. There are things on it called "apps." This is totally out of nowhere. Except that it's not. It's the direct result of about 25 years of Apple's entire philosophy and expertise.

What happens next? Blackberry's share of the smartphone market didn't drop immediately when the iPhone came out. In fact, it saw its biggest jumps yet, shooting all the way up from 8 percent to almost 20 percent of the global market by 2009. The first two years after the iPhone appeared were the two best years ever for Blackberry.[28]

But it went downhill fast from there. By the end of 2011, Blackberry had come all the way back down to 8 percent market share, where it had started when the iPhone launched. The release of the iPhone 3GS was a real breakthrough. The app store, and the whole concept of an app store, launched in 2008. The iPhone 3GS let tens of millions of new people join in. Apple was releasing a new model every fall, each one redefining what was possible.

The drop for Blackberry was astonishing. A mere two years later, by 2013, its market share was just 0.6 percent. Not 6 percent, mind

----

28　Statista Research Department, "Global Smartphone OS Market Share Held by RIM (BlackBerry) from 2007 to 2016, by Quarter," *Statista*, November 17, 2016, https://www.statista.com/statistics/263439/global-market-share-held-by-rim-smartphones/.

you. Zero point six percent. Just six in every thousand smartphones was a Blackberry.

It'd been buried in that avalanche of value creation. Blackberry had built a wonderful device that enabled you to do all the things you normally had to do in your office. You could check email, manage contacts, even web browse without having to be at your desk. Apple's iPhone enabled you to do all that plus a whole bunch of other things that you couldn't do before. Without the iPhone innovations, there would be no Uber. Without the iPhone, there would be no app store, commerce capabilities, great user interface, high-speed connectivity, and GPS. You can't have Uber without all of those. The iPhone 3GS brought them together. Without it, there is no Uber or a thousand other apps and services we now take for granted.

When you hear this story, who do you imagine yourself to be? Apple or Blackberry? Of course, everyone wants to be Apple, but it's not that simple. Blackberry was the leader, a pioneer, a trusted name. President Obama was a loyal customer well into the years where almost no one else was. Apple was a non-presence in the smartphone world. Of course, it had millions of customers and fans for the iPod and iMac. It was a big company in its own right, so it's not exactly a David and Goliath story.

The real contrast was where they started. Apple was on the outside, planning a revolution, and Blackberry was on top, growing its lead. In retrospect, we know what happened, but at the time, it was far from obvious.

The point here isn't to dance on Blackberry's grave or to sing hosannas to Apple. We've had plenty of both of those things. The point is to help people in the live entertainment business now. As the online events medium grows and develops, you need to know where you stand. It's a different opportunity based on where you are now. Both starting places have their own challenges and advantages. Apple was the revolutionary, and Blackberry was the counterrevolutionary.

Revolutionaries want change. Counterrevolutionaries want things to keep going the way they are. If the existing system nurtures or even protects your organization, you're a counterrevolutionary. If the existing system makes life hard for your organization, you're a potential revolutionary.

Smart revolutionaries look for ways to bring down the existing structure or perhaps take it over and then remodel it the way they want it. They use their insight and hustle to gain power and make change their friend. Smart counterrevolutionaries, though, don't just sit around in denial. They think about what could happen and try to beat the upstarts to the prize. They use their savvy and superior resources to make sure future change works for them.

You probably know which you are: revolutionary or counterrevolutionary. There's no exact play book, no guaranteed path to success for either. I do, however, have some rules to start your thinking, no matter which side you're on.

THREE RULES FOR ONLINE-EVENTS REVOLUTIONARIES

1. Live, breathe, and *be* your customer.

Revolutions are won when the revolutionaries end up on the same side as the people. The establishment sometimes forgets that you've got to wow the people who pay the bills. You can't forget this even for a moment. Even more, you've got to *lead* the people to what they want, especially the things they don't know they want yet. You can't do that without being completely immersed in what it means to be the people you're working for. Notice that I'm not saying, "Find out what people want, and give it to them." That's how the establishment thinks. I'm saying, **"Be one of the people, figure out what you want *next*, and deliver that."** There can be no compromise on this.

2. Don't play too nice.

Someday, you'll want acceptance from the elite members of the biz. Now's not the time to worry about that. Be ethical, civil, and constructive in your dealings with everybody, including the powerful. But don't go overboard. If they're not at least a little uncomfortable with you, it's either too early for them to see what's happening or you're not pushing hard enough.

3. Pay attention to new capabilities and put them to work.

Technological revolutions come from things we can do now that we didn't used to be able to do. Remember Uber's example and figure out what new thing is now possible. Even more important, figure out why that matters to the customer and deliver it (see Rule 1). You don't have to figure out how to be dominant right now. You just have to find a crack in the wall that you can gradually turn into a hole. Later, you'll make it big enough to drive a bus full of French-Canadian new-wave clowns through.

THREE RULES FOR ONLINE-EVENTS COUNTERREVOLUTIONARIES

1. Don't turn up your nose at things that people are doing that seem dumb to you.

Sure, there are fads, things that come and go. But if you're successful and powerful, or even just established, everything can seem like a fad. Let's face it: you want them to be fads. "New and popular" isn't really in the interest of people who more or less like things the way they are. I'm not accusing you of anything; it's just the truth about position. It may seem dumb, for example, that kids are watching other people play video games live on YouTube. It seems kinda dumb to me too, but I can tell you for sure that it's not a fad. It means a lot, and you can be sure that some people understand it well. They're ready to use that knowledge to create success, possibly at your expense. Pay attention. Suspend judgment. Assume that change is happening, and try to understand it *before* you judge it. In fact, understand it and don't judge it. Just use it.

2. Build your capabilities first.

You know how to measure success. You've got reliable metrics and methods. Resist the temptation to apply those methods to new things, including online events. That's because you'll never invest in the capabilities you need if you think this way. You'll look at the budget it takes to get a certain amount of revenue, and it won't come close to matching what you can do in your in-person business. This shouldn't surprise you. Online events are a new and emerging medium, and you're good at in-person events. After all, you've been doing them forever! You'd better be pretty good at the in-person thing by now. You're probably not that good at the online thing yet. It may be logical to measure the costs of time and money against the output of tickets and dollars. Logical, but wrong. It takes time and effort to get good at something, and the market for online events itself is still maturing. It reminds me of what Seth Godin says about learning to ride a unicycle. "All the time you're practicing, you aren't actually riding. You're *falling*. Then, if you don't give up after all this failure, in a blink, you're riding."[29] Focus on getting to the point where you're riding.

3. Follow fast and pour it on.
By hook or by crook, emulate the things that the revolutionaries are doing as quickly as you can. Hire them, hire someone who can do what they do, overspend in this area. And then, when you start to see success, step on the gas, throw in the kitchen sink, do not half-step. The revolutionaries might get there first, but that doesn't guarantee victory. There's an old saying that should give you some comfort: it's not who gets there first, it's who gets there *first with the most*. It's hard for an incumbent to be the most innovative. But it's a lot easier for an incumbent to copy that innovation and then send in the army!

It's hard to talk about Wild Card events because we don't know what they are. I almost didn't include this chapter. In the end, I felt a responsibility to leave it in because it's too important. As the pandemic eased up, I kept hearing about establishment types taking online events down a peg. It was an attempt to make the possibilities more comfortable for them. They talk about "digital content libraries" or "video captures" of their performances. They nod and say they see a "place" for online alongside in-person in the future.

But the emotional subtext of this is always pretty clear. "I want it to be small, contained, and secondary to what I know."

----

29 Seth Godin, "The Reason Riding a Unicycle Is Difficult," *Seth's Blog* (blog), July 26, 2009, https://seths.blog/2009/07/the-reason-riding-a-unicycle-is-difficult/.

Well, fine. I'm establishment enough to understand and sympathize with that feeling. But not everyone is. The live entertainment business is not facing an existential threat from online events. Quite the contrary, I think it's facing an existential windfall from online events. But not if people don't put them to use.

The only way online events could be an existential threat to the industry is if the right people ignore them. Let me correct that. There's no way to threaten the market for people who want to go out to shows.[30] But the industry that currently serves that market could be completely taken apart and rearranged. Remember the stories about the recording industry? Not fun.

But forget about that. There's absolutely no reason to allow a Napster-like scenario to play out. Digital live entertainment and arts have given our industry the gift of abundant opportunity. They're a supercharger on top of a business already going in the right direction.

Still, Wild Cards change the game, and you can be pretty sure they're lurking now in the world of online events.

THE GOLDEN FLOP

Here's one last Wild Card story that shows how change comes very gradually and then very suddenly.

In the 1960s, there was a gangly kid named Dick who went to high school in Oregon. He wanted to be on his high school's track team, but he didn't have a specialty. In those days, coaches encouraged kids to try everything and see what they liked. Dick was pretty terrible at most things. He wanted to be a sprinter because

---

30 Except a pandemic, as it turns out.

that's the glamor event, but he couldn't. The shot put weighed a ton, so he dropped that too.

But he was decent at the high jump. He barely made the cut, but he made it. He gutted it out and hung around the sport, determined to get better. Which he did.

In those days, most high jumpers used a technique called the Western Roll. To do this, you throw your lead leg up toward the bar like crazy. Then you roll your trailing leg over the bar afterwards. You'd usually land on your feet, possibly with one of your hands touching the ground, like a superhero.

Dick couldn't compete with the best guys in Oregon high school track. But he knew a little bit about physics. And he knew that competitions were now putting foam or big, soft landing pads on the other side of the high-jump bar. This would stop jumpers from hurting themselves when they landed.

This gave him an idea that he worked on. It made him a better and better jumper, and this continued for a few years.

Fast forward to the 1968 Olympics in Mexico City when Dick Fosbury defeated the best high jumpers in the world. His idea had become a Wild Card. He ran up to the bar, turned his back to it, sprang up high into the air with both legs, arched his back, kicked his legs, and landed face up on the safe, comforting foam on the other side.

Flop.

Undignified, but very effective.

They called it the Fosbury Flop, and it seemed to come from nowhere to win the Olympic Gold Medal. It turned a decent high jumper into the best in the world, and no one noticed it until it was too late to stop him.

Not only that, but by the next Olympics, most of the competitors were using his technique. And since then, it's become the standard. It changed the game that everyone was playing. It rearranged it, took it over, and literally elevated it.

That's the power of a Wild Card. Maybe there's one in your hand too.

CONCLUSION

I finished the draft of this book in July of 2021. I'd been writing it in pieces since fall of 2020. A lot had changed in the time, especially in the live industry. When I started writing, producers were cautiously starting to produce online events. In fact, there was a mini-boom in online events in late 2020 and early 2021. A bidding war for popular bands broke out. Pretty soon, people were making offers that meant they stood no chance to make money. It got a little stupid.

People had taken the most dysfunctional part of the concert business and brought it online. Thankfully, the madness didn't last long.

Not long after that, the pandemic began easing up. Producers started planning their return to in-person events. Hallelujah! It was like coming home after a long, hard journey.

But it wasn't that easy. Just getting back onstage would prove to be an ordeal of its own. Live event production and venue management is complex. It's not like a toaster that you can unplug, put away, and then plug back in when you need it. With the new post-Covid requirements, just getting back on stage would take precedence.

As a result, online events hit a lull. I was glad to see the online concert bubble pop, but I was not happy that so much of the smart investment stopped too.

One day, I was perusing the events on Stellar. The number had just started to grow again, and I noticed something. People were producing real, quality online events. They were innovating the new medium.

It was happening!

A university performing arts center in Nebraska was doing ride-along hybrid events for nearly everything it did onstage. A high-end cabaret in California was streaming professional music concerts several times a week. A major movie studio was planning a series of "co-watching" events like the ones we'd seen earlier in the year. I saw a lot of new online-first events that also had paying audiences. Two or three organizations were producing recurring personality-based talk shows, building an audience for their brands. There were circuses and kids shows and experimental theatre. There were schools and celebrities and nonprofits. There were obvious crowd-pleasers and artsy stuff that would probably find a niche audience, if it found one at all.

It all had the feel of something beginning. Something being born.

I wrote this book to achieve three things.

- To show you *why* you should be doing online events.

- To give you a start on *how* to do online events.

- To help you understand *what* you can create in this new medium.

If you're a live event producer or have an ambition to be, don't ignore this opportunity. It's an industry-shaking reset moment. And you get to be there at the beginning.

I hope you saw in the first part of the book how important it is to think in terms of *scale* when approaching online events. There are so many people out there who might be fans of what you've got to show them. Yes, live entertainment is saddled with a tough business model—the Business Model of the Damned—but online events help you overcome that.

In Part 2, I showed you how to think practically about starting online events. Before you do anything, I want you to *respect the medium* itself and think about it the right way. Many have fallen into the trap of not starting here. Once you respect the medium, you need to *master the technology*, which isn't as hard as you may think. If you take both of these steps, you'll still need a *marketing plan that works for an online event*. Finally, you can always go back and reference my Big 5 steps for online event success.

The third part of the book focused on the kinds of online events you should consider. I outlined the strengths, weaknesses, and characteristics of all of them. I distinguished between online-only, ride-along hybrid, and online-first hybrid events. These chapters can help you decide what kind of events you should be doing. Remember that there are still Wild Cards waiting to be played. These are the ones that are going to change everything, even if we don't know what they are yet. Whether you're a disruptor or an incumbent, you need to understand Wild Cards. Because they're out there, just waiting to be invented.

If I could make a wish and have it come true, I'd wish for you to feel ready to start. I'd wish for what I've shared to give you the confidence and knowledge to get to work on your online events. I'd wish for these pages to be the cornerstone of a great and successful career with online events. I'd wish for you to have people all around the world thrilled to watch what you're creating. I'd wish for you to be successful and happy as you reach even more people with your events.

It's more than just a wish, of course. If you want to get started, and I can be of help, just ask! Go to http://www.WorkWithStellar.com and drop us a line. Or email me directly at jmccarthy@stellar.live. My job is to help you get this right!

This is a small book because I can't teach you most of what you need to know. Your success is going to be your own, and it will come from days and months and years of hard work and persistence. It's a path you'll make for yourself.

I only hope I've helped point you in the right direction.

CPSIA information can be obtained
at www.ICGtesting.com
Printed in the USA
LVHW100628290922
729560LV00014B/241/J

9 781544 531076